煤炭高等教育"十三五"规划教材

【学者文库】

信息科学英语

吕茂丽　唐建敏◎主编

吉林大学出版社
·长春·

图书在版编目（CIP）数据

信息科学英语 / 吕茂丽，唐建敏主编 .—长春：吉林大学出版社，2020.2
ISBN 978-7-5692-6139-4

Ⅰ.①信… Ⅱ.①吕…②唐… Ⅲ.①信息学—英语 Ⅳ.①G201

中国版本图书馆 CIP 数据核字（2020）第 030201 号

书　　名	信息科学英语 XINXI KEXUE YINGYU
作　　者	吕茂丽　唐建敏　主编
策划编辑	李潇潇
责任编辑	赵雪君
责任校对	刘　丹
装帧设计	中联华文
出版发行	吉林大学出版社
社　　址	长春市人民大街 4059 号
邮政编码	130021
发行电话	0431-89580028/29/21
网　　址	http：//www.jlup.com.cn
电子邮箱	jdcbs@jlu.edu.cn
印　　刷	三河市华东印刷有限公司
开　　本	710mm×1000mm　1/16
印　　张	12.5
字　　数	160 千字
版　　次	2021 年 1 月第 1 版
印　　次	2021 年 1 月第 1 次
书　　号	ISBN 978-7-5692-6139-4
定　　价	95.00 元

版权所有　翻印必究

编委会

主　编：吕茂丽　唐建敏

副主编：张卫东　徐育新　崔雪红　杨晨晨

　　　　　韩　梅　刘炳淑　杨　明　赵才华

前　言

根据《大学英语教学指南》的精神,大学英语的课程体系主要由通用英语、专门用途英语和跨文化交际三大部分组成。本教材充分体现新时期大学英语教学的要求,以培养学生的学术英语能力和应用能力为目标,将专业英语的学科内容与英语语言学习相结合,满足新时期国家和社会对人才培养的需要。

本教材以内容为依托的教学理念为编写思路,具有针对性、实用性和时代性。教材所选内容与信息科学学科专业密切相关,包括了信息科学学科的基本知识和前沿信息,选材地道真实,内容丰富,信息量大。同时考虑学生的真实水平,从学生的实际需要出发,能够实现向专业英语学习平稳过渡,满足了不同专业学生未来就业的需求。在当前信息化社会的新形势下,选材具有强烈的时代气息,兼具专业性和趣味性,有利于激发学生学习英语的兴趣并拓宽和提升学生的信息素养。

本教材以语言运用培养为主线,以学术内容为基础,主题选材与信息科学类学科有关,采用主题模式,有效融入了学科专业知识。教材内容分为8个单元,每个单元围绕一个主题展开,每一单元同时与其他单元有一定的关联,涉及操作系统、软件工程、互联网、电子商务、人机交互、大数据、人工智能和虚拟环境主题。每个单元分为三个部分,即第一部分为学术英语阅读技巧;第二部分为课内阅读 Passage A 和课外阅读 Passage B;第三部分为学术英语写作训练。每篇文章长度在 1000～1500 字左右,后附有单词表和相关课后练习,练习设计与单元阅读技巧和单元主题密切相关,通过设计各种阅读、写作和翻译训练,指导学生进行信息的查找、总结和评价分析,帮助学生在今后的学习和工作中较好地交流和获取信息,以培养学生在专业领域的语言应用能力和批判性思维能力。

随着计算机技术的应用,在全球展开的信息技术革命正以前所未有的方式对社会变革的方向起着决定作用。大学生应该掌握在信息化社会里工作、学习和生活所必须具备的计算机基础知识,系统地建立相关概念,具备获取知识和交流的能力。因此,本书适用于修完大学英语基础课程,达到一般要求水平的理工类院校本科生,提升学生的信息素养和语言应用能力。本书尤其适用于信息科学学科的本科生和研究生,提高学生的英语综合语言技能,并为学生专业需求学习服务。本书可供一个学期使用,参考教学时间为 32 学时。教师可根据实际需要选择教学内容,制定个性化的教学方案。

在本书的编写过程中,参考了部分国内外相关书籍和网站,如有疏漏敬请谅解,并在此向相关作者表示衷心的感谢。

由于编者水平有限,疏漏不当之处在所难免,敬请读者批评指正。

编者
2019 年 5 月

目 录
CONTENTS

Unit 1 Operating System ·········· 1

    Passage A What Is an Operating System? ·········· 2

    Passage B Real-Time Operating System (RTOS) ·········· 13

Unit 2 Software Engineering ·········· 24

    Passage A What Is Software Engineering? ·········· 25

    Passage B Application and System Software ·········· 36

Unit 3 Internet ·········· 50

    Passage A What Is Internet? ·········· 51

    Passage B Computer Network ·········· 63

Unit 4 Electronic Business ·········· 75

    Passage A Ecommerce ·········· 76

Passage B　Hot Trends That Will Continue to Change Your Ecommerce Horizons in 2018 ················· 87

Unit 5　Human-Computer Interaction ························· 99
　　Passage A　Human-Machine Interaction ················· 100
　　Passage B　Human-Machine Interaction Now And in the Future ·· 111

Unit 6　Big Data ··· 120
　　Passage A　Creating Value in Health Care Through Big Data ·· 121
　　Passage B　Big Data and Its Application ················· 135

Unit 7　Artificial Intelligence ······································ 146
　　Passage A　What Is Artificial Intelligence? ··············· 147
　　Passage B　Benefits & Risks of Artificial Intelligence ········· 158

Unit 8　Virtual Environment ······································ 167
　　Passage A　Virtual Reality ································· 168
　　Passage B　How Reality Technology Is Used in Business? ·· 181

Unit 1   Operating System

Part One Academic Reading Skills

Skimming

Skimming is a fast reading strategy, which refers to the process of reading only for the gist (or main idea) within a passage to get an overall impression of the content. It is usually done at a speed three to four times faster than normal reading. When skimming you ignore the details and only look for the gist.

The following tips will be helpful:

1. Look at the title, subtitles, and illustrations to predict the topic of the passage. Read each subtitle and find the relationships among them.

2. Glance quickly through the first and the last paragraphs to identify the general topic of the passage.

3. Identify signal words concerning the development of the ideas, such as *"in addition"*, *"next"*, *"we can conclude"* and so on.

4. Read the titles of tables, graphs, figures, diagrams or other overt information. Notice any numerations, italicized or boldface words or expressions.

Part Two Passage Reading

Passage A   What Is an Operating System?

Pre-reading Task

Directions: *Read the title and discuss the following questions in groups.*

1. How much do you know about operating systems?

2. What can operation systems provide?

Defining OS

An operating system (OS) refers to the program that manages a computer's resources, especially the allocation of those resources among other programs. Typical resources include the central processing unit (CPU), computer memory, file storage, input/output (I/O) devices, and network connections. Management tasks include scheduling resource use to avoid conflicts and interference between programs. Unlike most programs, which complete a task and terminate, an operating system runs indefinitely and terminates only when the computer is turned off.

Multiprocessing OS

Modern multiprocessing operating systems allow many processes to be active, where each process is a "thread" of computation being used to execute a program. One form of multiprocessing is called time-sharing, which lets many users share computer access by rapidly switching between them. Time-sharing must guard against interference between users' programs, and most systems use virtual memory. This virtual memory both increases the address space available to a program and helps to prevent programs from interfering with each other, but it requires careful control by the operating system and a set of allocation tables to keep track of memory use. Perhaps the most delicate and critical task for a modern operating system is allocation of the CPU; each process is allowed to use the CPU for a limited time, which may be a fraction of a second, and then must give up control and become suspended until its next turn. Switching between processes must itself use the CPU while protecting all data of the processes.

History of OS

The first digital computers had no operating systems. They ran one program at a time, which had command of all system resources, and a human operator would provide any special resources needed. The first operating systems were developed in the mid-1950s. These were small "supervisor programs" that provided basic I/O operations (such as controlling punch card readers and printers) and kept accounts of CPU usage for billing. Supervisor programs also provided multiprogramming capabilities to enable several programs to run at once. This was particularly important so that these early multimillion-dollar machines would not be idle during slow I/O operations.

Computers acquired more powerful operating systems in the 1960s with the emergence of time-sharing, which required a system to manage multiple users sharing CPU time and terminals. Two early time-sharing systems were CTSS (Compatible Time Sharing System), developed at the Massachusetts Institute of Technology, and the Dartmouth College Basic System, developed at Dartmouth College. Other multi-programmed systems included Atlas, at the University of Manchester, England, and IBM's OS/360, probably the most complex software package of the 1960s. After 1972 the Multics system for General Electric Co.'s GE 645 computer (and later for Honeywell Inc.'s computers) became the most sophisticated system, with most of the multi-programming and time-sharing capabilities that later became standard.

The minicomputers of the 1970s had limited memory and required smaller operating systems. The most important operating system of that period was UNIX, developed by AT&T for large minicomputers as a simpler alternative to Multics. It became widely used in the 1980s, in part because it was free to universities and in part because it was designed with a set of tools that were powerful in the hands of skilled programmers. More recently, Linux, an open-source version of UNIX developed in part by a group led by Finnish computer science student Linus Torvalds and in part by a group led by American computer programmer Richard Stallman, has become popular on personal computers as well as on larger computers.

In addition to such general-purpose systems, special-purpose operating systems run on small computers that control assembly lines, aircraft, and even home appliances. They are real-time systems, designed to provide rapid response to sensors and to use their inputs to control machinery. Operating systems have also been developed for mobile devices such as smartphones and tablets. Apple Inc.'s iOS, which runs on iPhones and iPads, and Google Inc.'s Android are two prominent mobile operating systems.

What does OS provide?

From the standpoint of a user or an application program, an operating system provides services. Some of these are simple user commands like "dir"—show the files on a disk—while others are low-level "system calls" that a graphics program might use to display an image. In either case the operating system provides appropriate access to its objects, the tables of disk locations in one case and the routines to transfer data to the screen in the other. Some of its routines, those that manage the CPU and memory, are generally accessible only to other portions of the operating system.

Contemporary operating systems for personal computers commonly provide a graphical user interface (GUI). The GUI may be an intrinsic part of the system, as in the older versions of Apple's Mac OS and Microsoft Corporation's Windows OS; in others it is a set of programs that depend on an underlying system, as in the X Window system for UNIX and Apple's Mac OS X.

Operating systems also provide network services and file-sharing capabilities—even the ability to share resources between systems of different types, such as Windows and UNIX. Such sharing has become feasible through the introduction of network protocols (communication rules) such as the Internet's TCP/IP.

(Total words:901,taken from:https://www.britannica.com)

New Words and Expressions

allocation /ˌæləˈkeɪʃən/ n. an amount of something, especially money, that is given to a particular person or used for a particular purpose(尤指经费) 配置,分配

scheduling resource 调度资源

interference /ˌɪntəˈfɪər(ə)ns/ n. unwanted or unnecessary involvement in something 干扰

computation /ˌkɒmpjʊˈteɪʃ(ə)n/ n. mathematical calculation 计算

terminate /ˈtɜːmɪneɪt/ v. ends completely 结束,终止

indefinitely /ɪnˈdefɪnətli/ adv. to an indefinite extent 无限期地

execute /ˈeksɪkjuːt/ v. carry out or perform an action 执行

guard /ɡɑːd/ n. a device designed to prevent injury or accidents 防护装置 v. watch over or shield from danger or harm, protect 保卫,监视

virtual /ˈvɜːtʃuəl/ adj. generated by a computer to simulate real objects and activities 虚拟的

reside in 存在于,驻留

keep track of 跟踪;记录

delicate /ˈdelɪkət/ adj. exquisitely fine and subtle and pleasing 微妙

的

fraction /ˈfrækʃ(ə)n/ n. a small part or item forming a piece of a whole 一小部分

suspended /səˈspendɪd/ adj. (of undissolved particles in a fluid) supported or kept from sinking or falling by buoyancy and without apparent attachment 悬浮的；暂停的

punch /pʌn(t)ʃ/ v. touch them in order to store information on a machine such as a computer or to give the machine a command to do something; make holes in it by pushing or pressing it with something sharp 按键；打孔

idle /ˈaɪdl/ adj. not in action or at work 闲置的

sophisticated /səˈfɪstɪkeɪtɪd/ adj. complex 复杂的

assembly line(工厂产品的)装配线

sensor /ˈsensə(r)/ n. any device that receives a signal or stimulus (as heat or pressure or light or motion etc.) and responds to it in a distinctive manner 传感器

standpoint /ˈstændpɔɪnt/ n. a mental position from which things are viewed 立场，观点

contemporary /kənˈtemprəri/ adj. characteristic of the present 现代的

intrinsic /ɪnˈtrɪnsɪk/ adj. situated within or belonging solely to the organ or body part on which it acts 固有的

feasible /ˈfiːzəbl/ adj. capable of being done with means at hand and circumstances as they are 可行的

protocol /ˈprəʊtəkɒl/ n. (computer science) rules determining the format and transmission of data 协议,草案;礼仪

Proper Nouns

  OS operating system 操作系统

  CPU central processing unit 中央处理器

  computer memory 计算机内存

  file storage 文件存储器

  I/O devices 输入输出设备

  magnetic hard disk drive 硬磁盘驱动器

  CTSS compatible time sharing system 兼容分时系统

  GUI graphical user interface 图形用户界面

  IP Internet Protocol 互联网协议

  dir 显示文件列表

Reading Task

Task 1 Skim Passage A for the following questions.

1. Look at the title and predict the main contents of the passage.

2. If you want to get some information about the development of OS in 1960s, to which subtitle should you refer?

3. Which subtitle is about the benefits we gain from OS?

Task 2 Skim Passage A and identify the paragraphs which contain the information.

1. The first operating systems were supervisor programs which enabled several programs to run at once. (　　)

2. Operating system manages the allocation of computer resources. Typical resources include CPU, computer memory, file storage, I/O devices, and network connections. (   )

3. Time-sharing, one form of multiprocessing, lets many users share computer access by rapidly switching between them. (   )

Task 3 Complete the following table about the history of OS.

The history of operating system	In the mid-1950s, supervisor programs not only _____ and kept accounts of CPU usage for billing, but also _____ to enable several programs to run at once.
	Thanks to the supervisor program, the early multimillion-dollar machines would not be _____ during slow I/O operations.
	In the 1960s, with the emergence of time-sharing, computers had powerful operating systems, which required a system to _____ multiple users _____ and _____.
	After 1972, _____ system for General Electric Co.'s GE 645 computer become the most _____ system.
	In the 1970s, the most important operating system was _____, which was developed by _____ for large minicomputers as a simpler alternative to Multics.
	In the 1980s, UNIX became widely used, not only because it was _____ but also because it was _____ a set of tools that were powerful in the hands of skilled programmers.
	Real-time systems designed to provide _____ to sensors and to use their _____ to control machinery.
	In addition to these systems, mobile devices also developed _____ operating system, such as iOS and Android.

Task 4 Decide whether the following statements are true (T) or false (F).

1. Like most programs, which complete a task and terminate, an operating system also stops running at any time. (   )

2. The first digital computers had no operating systems. (   )

3. The first operating systems were developed in the mid-1940s. (   )

4. Computers acquired more powerful operating systems in the 1960s with the emergence of real-time system, which required a system to manage multiple users sharing CPU time and terminals. (   )

5. Real-time systems designed to provide rapid response to sensors and to use their inputs to control machinery. (   )

6. The minicomputer had limited memory, so they need small operating system. (   )

Task 5 Work in pairs and answer the following questions.

1. Why are the supervisor programs' multiprogramming capabilities particularly important?

2. "Other multiprogrammed systems included Atlas, at the University of Manchester, England, and IBM's OS/360, probably the most complex software package of the 1960s. " (Para. 4) Why does the author use "probably" to describe the sentence?

3. Why did UNIX become widely used in the 1980s?

Task 6 Group Discussion

Nowadays, when you purchase a mobile device the manufacturer will have chosen the operating system for that specific device. Such as Apple Inc.'s iOS which runs on iPhones and iPads and Google Inc.'s Android which runs on other smartphones. Work in groups of 3—4 and discuss the following questions.

How do you comment on the two mobile operating systems? In addition to these two mobile operating systems, do you know more mobile operating systems? List more mobile operating systems.

Language Building-up

Task 1 The following expressions are taken from Text A. Translate the following terms from English into Chinese.

network protocols

indefinitely

execute

virtual

keep track of

feasible

Task 2 Match each word with the best definition.

interference	belonging to or part of the real nature of sth./sb.
terminate	delay or stop
fraction	possible and likely to be achieved
sophisticated	for a period of time with no fixed limit
intrinsic	to do a piece of work, perform a duty

11

virtual	complicated
execute	a small part or amount of sth.
feasible	interruption
indefinitely	end
suspend	made to appear to exist by the use of computer software

Task 3 Complete the following sentences with the correct form of the words and expressions in the box.

feasible   indefinitely   execute   keep track of   virtual   terminate

1. The App life cycle is the progress of an App from its launch through its _____.

2. The meeting's postponed _____.

3. We are going to _____ our campaign plan to the letter.

4. One day _____ reality will revolutionize the entertainment industry.

5. Police _____ the kidnapper using electronic surveillance equipment.

6. The committee will study the _____ of setting up a national computer network.

Task 4 Translate the following paragraph into English.

Android 是一种基于 Linux 的操作系统,主要使用于移动设备,如智能手机和平板电脑。Android 操作系统最初由 Andy Rubin 开发,主要支持手机。2005 年 8 月由 Google 收购。2007 年 11 月,Google 与 84 家硬件制造商、软件开发商及电信营运商组建开放手机联盟(Open Handset

Alliance)共同研发改良 Android 系统。第一部 Android 智能手机发布于 2008 年 10 月。Android 逐渐扩展到平板电脑及其他领域上,如电视、数码相机、游戏机、智能手表等。全世界采用这款系统的设备数量已经达到 10 亿。

Passage B　Real-Time Operating System（RTOS）

What Is a Real-Time Operating System（RTOS）?

A real-time operating system（RTOS）is an operating system that works in real time, with deterministic constraints that require efficient time usage and power to process incoming data and relay the expected results without any unknown or unexpected delays. RTOS software is time dependent, which means that it should process input and offer output within a short predetermined deterministic period. However the key to an RTOS, and the most important demand of RTOS software is that a request and response for data is guaranteed to occur. If a Windows OS has request and response calls that are fast 90% of the time, yet the remaining 10% of the time an input/output request takes too long, then the real-time application is not performing correctly. Thus an RTOS is not meant to be only fast, it is more importantly meant to be dependable.

Components of an RTOS

A real-time operating system includes multiple components:

The scheduler. This is the main RTOS element that determines the order of execution of tasks or threads usually based on a priority scheme, and either in a run to completion or round robin fashion. Some RTOS may try to load balance thread across processors but most require developers to assign process affinity to cores to optimize real-time application resource usage.

Symmetric Multiprocessing (SMP). An RTOS has the ability to handle and separate multiple tasks or threads so that they can be run on multiple cores to allow for parallel processing of code (i. e. multitasking).

Function library. It is a standard interface that can contain an application program interface (API) to call routines within it. It is also the interface that connects that application code and the kernel. Application code entities direct requests to the kernel via the function library to prompt the application to give the desired programmatic behavior.

Dispatch latency. Dispatch latency describes the amount of time it takes for a system to respond to a request for a process to begin operation. With a scheduler written specifically to honor application priorities, real-time applications can be developed with a bounded dispatch latency.

User-defined data objects and classes. An RTOS relies on programming languages with data structures that are organized based on their type of operation. The user defines object sets through a specified programming language like C++ that the RTOS will use in to control the specified application.

Memory management. Memory management is required to allocate memory for every program. In an RTOS, this is important, since unlike General Purpose OSes like Windows, it can't afford to have memory paged in or out since it leads to non-deterministic behavior.

Types of Real-Time Operating Systems

Real-time operating systems are classified into two types:

Soft real-time systems. Meeting command deadlines in soft real-time operating systems is not compulsory for every task. However, the systems should always give the expected results. A soft RTOS requires that a response be logically correct and occur before a certain deadline or the result becomes increasingly inaccurate. Essentially the result can still hold some value even though it occurred after the required deadline.

Hard real-time systems. A hard real-time system is a time constrained and deterministic system that responds within a specified time frame. They are dictated by deadlines, latency and time constraints. For instance, if an output is expected within 10 seconds, the system should process the input and give out the output by the 10th second. Note that the output should not be released by the 9th or 11th second to prevent the system from failing.

Applications of Real-Time Operating Systems

An RTOS can be flexible but is usually designed for set purposes. Most RTOS subsystems are assigned certain tasks and leave anything and everything else not designated to it for the Windows OS itself to handle. An RTOS offers mostly operational solutions, including applications such as:

Control systems. The RTOS is used to monitor and execute control system commands. Real-time systems are used to control actuators and sensors for functions like digital controllers. Controlled systems include aircraft, brakes, and engines. Controlled systems are monitored with the help of sensors and altered by actuators. The RTOS reads the data from sensors and then performs calculations and moves the actuators so that movement in a flight can be simulated.

Image processing. Computers, mobile gadgets, and cameras must achieve their intended duty in real time, which means that visual input is needed in real-time with the utmost precision so that industrial automation, for instance can control what is happening on conveyors or an assembly line when an item is moving down its path and there is a defect, or the item has moved its location. Real-time image processing is essential for making real-time adjustments for moving objects.

Voice over IP (VoIP). VoIP relies on Internet protocols to transmit voices in real time. As such, VoIP can be implemented on any IP network like intranets, local area networks, and the Internet. The voice is digitalized, compressed and converted to IP packets in real time before being transmitted over an IP network.

Considerations for Choosing an RTOS

Is an RTOS right for your computing needs? Consider the following factors.

Performance. Performance is a core factor that must be considered when choosing an RTOS. Real-time operating systems are different and perform differently. Key aspect for an RTOS is that its determinism guarantees that request and responses of data happen within a set period of time no matter what else is happening in the PC system. When determining the best RTOS, ask questions such as whether the system is showing any jitter within your tolerance range and thereby providing the determinism that you need. RTOS performance should be determined by a system's dependence on executing calls within a specified period, regardless of anything else happening on the system.

Unique features. Every real-time operating system has unique features that determine how it operates to execute commands. As such, you must evaluate the features required to run your system effectively and choose an RTOS with the relevant features. A good RTOS should be scalable and feature efficient memory protection systems.

Your IT team. Most people overlook their IT team when selecting the ideal RTOS. A good RTOS should favor your IT team by reducing their labor intensity so they have more time to focus on product differentiators and learn how to setup and integrate a real-time operating system. So, decide on an RTOS that your IT team is familiar with and can work with.

Middleware. Almost all real-time operating systems feature middleware components or third-party components that are integrated with the RTOS. You should evaluate the middleware to ensure that it has a seamless integration method. If your RTOS lacks middleware support, you may have to deal with time-consuming integration processes. Ensure that your middleware features components like TCP/IP and file systems.

A real-time operating system should be of premium quality and easy to navigate. Developing embedded projects is hard and time-consuming; developers should not have to struggle with real-time system-related issues that can be distracting. An RTOS should be a trusted component that any developer can count on.

(Total words:1192, taken from: https://www. intervalzero. com)

New Words and Expressions

predetermine /priːdɪˈtɜːmɪn/ vt. & vi. determine beforehand 预先裁定，注定

affinity /əˈfɪnəti/ n. a close connection marked by community of interests or similarity in nature or character 密切关系，类似

function library 函数库

dispatch latency 调度延迟

trigger /ˈtrɪɡə(r)/ vt. 引发，触发

preempt /priˈempt/ vt. 先占，先发制人，先取，取代

constrain /kənˈstreɪn/ v. lacking spontaneity 约束，限制

time frame 时帧

dictate /dɪkˈteɪt/ vt. issue commands or orders for 口述；命令，指示；使听写；控制

constraint /kənˈstreɪnt/ n. the act of constraining 约束；限制；强制

actuator /ˈæktʃʊeɪtə/ n. a mechanism that puts something into automatic action 执行器

brake /breɪk/ n. a restraint used to slow or stop a vehicle 刹车

engine /ˈendʒɪn/ n. motor that converts thermal energy to mechanical work 发动机,引擎

simulate /ˈsɪmjuleɪt/ vt. make a pretence of 模拟,模仿

gadget /ˈgædʒɪt/ n. a device or control that is very useful for a particular job 装置

utmost /ˈʌtməʊst/ adj. highest in extent or degree 极度的,最大的

precision /prɪˈsɪʒn/ n. the quality of being reproducible in amount or performance 精确度

implement /ˈɪmplɪment/ vt. pursue to a conclusion or bring to a successful issue 实现

intranet /ˈɪntrənet/ n. 内联网

compress /kəmˈpres/ v. squeeze or press together 压缩

performance /pəˈfɔːməns/ n. 性能

jitter /ˈdʒɪtə/ n. small rapid variations in a waveform resulting from fluctuations in the voltage supply or mechanical vibrations or other sources 抖动

scalable /ˈskeɪləbl/ adj. capable of being scaled 可升级的

differentiator /ˌdɪfəˈrenʃɪeɪtə/ n. one who (or that which) differentiates 区分者,微分器

setup /ˈsetʌp/ n. the way something is organized or arranged 设置,计划

integrate /ˈɪntɪgreɪt/ v. make into a whole or make part of a whole 集成，使一体化

seamless /ˈsiːmləs/ adj. perfectly consistent and coherent 无缝的，无漏洞的

premium /ˈpriːmiəm/ adj. having or reflecting superior quality or value 优质的

navigate /ˈnævɪgeɪt/ vt. direct carefully and safely 导航；航行，驾驶

embedded /ɪmˈbedɪd/ adj. inserted as an integral part of a surrounding whole 嵌入式的

Proper Nouns

  RTOS real-time operating system 实时操作系统

  SMP Symmetric Multiprocessing 对称多处理，也译为均衡多处理、对称性多重处理

  API application program interface 应用程序接口

  VoIP Voice over Internet Protocol IP网络中的语音传输

Reading Task

Task 1 Skim Passage B for the following questions.

1. Which subtitle can we find suggestions for choosing an RTOS?

2. Which subtitle is about the constituent parts of an RTOS?

3. Which subtitle defines RTOS?

Task 2 Skim the passage and determine which subtitles that the following statements correspond with.

1. RTOS software works in real time and is time dependent.

2. RTOS comprises many components, including SMP, function library, dispatch latency, etc...

3. Hard real-time system is time constrained and dictated by deadlines.

4. The voice is processed before being transmitted over an IP network.

5. Middleware should have seamless integration method.

Task 3 Skim the passage and fill in the summary.

In choosing an RTOS, _____ is a core factor that must be considered. Also, consider _____ because that determines how it operates to execute commands. Most people overlook their _____ when selecting the ideal RTOS. A good RTOS should favor your IT team by reducing their labor intensity. Lastly, your RTOS cannot lack _____ because they are integrated with RTOS.

Language Building-up

Task 1 Translate the following sentences from the passage into Chinese.

1. The heightened reliance on technology to execute crucial tasks led to the development of high-performance and deterministic operating systems, including real-time operating systems (RTOS).

2. A good RTOS should favor your IT team by reducing their labor intensity so they have more time to focus on product differentiators and learn how to setup and integrate a real-time operating system.

3. Almost all real-time operating systems feature middleware components or third-party components that are integrated with the RTOS.

4. This software is designed to serve as a hard real-time system that delivers output within a specified time frame to improve embedded systems' quality.

Task 2 Paraphrase the following sentences from the passage.

1. A real-time operating system should be of premium quality and easy to navigate.

2. Most people overlook their IT team when selecting the ideal RTOS.

3. Every real-time operating system has unique features that determine how it operates to execute commands.

4. Performance is a core factor that must be considered when choosing an RTOS.

Part Three Academic Writing

Theme-related Writing

On the basis of what you have learned from this unit, write an essay entitled "The Prospect of Real-Time Operating System". You should write at least 150 words but no more than 200 words.

Unit 2　Software Engineering

Part One　Academic Reading Skills

Scanning

Scanning means to look quickly and not very thoroughly through a text to locate a specific fact or piece of information. For example, if you want to find the definition of certain term, consult the part which contains the specific and relevant information and disregard other parts which do not contain it. Thus your reading should be more efficient and quicker. Scanning is a fast reading method which helps you to find specific information quickly.

When you are scanning, you know the words you are scanning for. Or you have a question in your mind and you read a passage only to find the answer. Unrelated information is ignored in this process.

How to scan? The following steps may be of help:

1. Decide what information you are looking for and keep it in your mind all the time.

2. Spot key words carrying clues of the passage. Pay attention to the numbers, proper names, and abbreviations in targeted questions.

3. Analyze the organization of the content before starting to scan. If the material is familiar and brief, you may scan the whole passage to search the information you need. If the material is difficult and long, you may need to do some skimming to determine which part to scan.

4. Once determined, you may move your eyes as fast as you can to find the information.

Part Two Passage Reading

Passage A What Is Software Engineering?

Pre-reading Task

Directions: *Read the title and discuss the following questions in groups.*

1. Why has Java been known as a high-level language?

2. Why do manufacturers require the whole process to be entirely managed by software engineers?

3. From the perspective of software engineering, can you explain the development process of iOS on iPhones and iPads?

Software engineering treats the approach to developing software as a formal process much like that found in traditional engineering. Software engineers begin by analyzing user needs. They design software, deploy, test it for quality and maintain it. They instruct computer programmers how to write the code they need. Software engineers may or may not write any of the code themselves, but they need strong programming skills to communicate with the programmers and are frequently fluent in several programming languages.

Software engineers design and develop computer games, business applications, network control systems and software operating systems. They are experts in the theory of computing software and the limitations of the hardware they design for.

Computer-Aided Software Engineering

The whole software design process has to be formally managed long before the first line of code is written. Software engineers produce lengthy design documents using computer-aided software engineering tools. The software engineer then converts the design documents into design specification documents, which are used to design code. The process is organized and efficient. There is no off-the-cuff programming going on.

Paperwork

One distinguishing feature of software engineering is the paper trail that it produces. Designs are signed off by managers and technical authorities, and the role of quality assurance is to check the paper trail. Many software engineers admit that their job is 70 percent paperwork and 30 percent code. It's a costly but responsible way to write software, which is one reason why avionics in modern aircraft are so expensive.

Software Engineering Challenges

Manufacturers cannot build complex life-critical systems like aircraft, nuclear reactor controls, and medical systems and expect the software to be thrown together. They require the whole process to be thoroughly managed by software engineers so that budgets can be estimated, staff recruited and the risk of failure or expensive mistakes minimized.

In safety-critical areas such as aviation, space, nuclear power plants, medicine, fire detection systems, and roller coaster rides, the cost of software failure can be enormous because lives are at risk. The ability of the software engineer to anticipate problems and eliminate them before they happen is critical.

Certification and Education

In some parts of the world and in most U.S. states, you cannot call yourself a software engineer without a formal education or certification. Several of the large software companies, including Microsoft, Oracle and Red Hat offer courses toward certifications. Many colleges and universities offer degrees in software engineering. Aspiring software engineers may major in computer science, software engineering, mathematics or computer information systems.

Computer Programmers

Programmers write code to the specifications given to them by software engineers. They are experts in the major computer programming languages. Although they aren't usually involved in the early design stages, they may be involved in testing, modifying, updating and repairing the code. They write code in one or more of the in-demand programming languages, including: SQL, Java, C++, Python, PHP, Ruby on Rails, Objective-C, etc.

The Structured Query Language (SQL) is the language of databases. All modern relational databases, including Access, FileMaker Pro, Microsoft SQL Server and Oracle use SQL as their basic building block. In fact, it's often the only way that you can interact with the database itself. All of the graphical user interfaces that provide data entry and manipulation functionality are nothing more than SQL translators. They take the actions you perform graphically and convert them to SQL commands understood by the database.

Java is a computer programming language. It enables programmers to write computer instructions using English-based commands instead of having to write in numeric codes. It's known as a high-level language because it can be read and written easily by humans. Like English, Java has a set of rules that determine how the instructions are written. These rules are known as its syntax. Once a program has been written, the high-level instructions are translated into numeric codes that computers can understand and execute.

C++ is a general purpose object-oriented programming language developed at Microsoft and released in 2002. It is similar to Java in its syntax. The purpose of C++ is to precisely define a series of operations that a computer can perform to accomplish a task. Most C++ operations involve manipulating numbers and text, but anything that the computer can physically do can be programmed in C++. Computers have no intelligence—they have to be told exactly what to do, and their actions are defined by the programming language you use. Once programmed, they can repeat the steps as many times as needed at high speed. Modern PCs are so fast they can count to a billion in seconds.

Python is a general-purpose programming language that can be used on any modern computer operating system. It can be used for processing text, numbers, images, scientific data and just about anything else you might save on a computer. It is used daily in the operations of the Google search engine, the video-sharing website YouTube, NASA and the New York Stock Exchange. These are but a few of the places where Python plays important roles in the success of the business, government, and non-profit organizations; there are many others.

PHP is a server side scripting language used on the Internet to create dynamic web pages. It is often coupled with MySQL, a relational database server that can store the information and variables the PHP files may use. Together they can create everything from the simplest web site to a full blown business web site, an interactive web forum, or even an online role playing game.

Ruby is unique among object-oriented scripting languages. In a sense, it's a purist's language for those who love object-oriented languages. Everything, without exception, is automatically an object, whereas in other programming languages this isn't true. Ruby's architect Yukihiro Matsumoto designed the language to be simple enough for beginning programmers to use while also powerful enough for experienced programmers to have all the tools they'd need. It sounds contradictory, but this dichotomy is owed to Ruby's pure object-oriented design and Matsumoto's careful selection of features from other languages such as Perl, Smalltalk, and Lisp. There are libraries for building all types of applications with Ruby: XML parsers, GUI bindings, networking protocols, game libraries and more. Ruby programmers also have access to the powerful RubyGems program. Comparable to Perl's CPAN, RubyGems makes it easy to import other programmers' libraries into your own programs.

Developed over 30 years ago, Objective-C was backwards compatible with C but incorporated elements of the programming language Smalltalk. In 1988 Steve Jobs founded NeXT and they licensed Objective-C. NeXT was acquired by Apple in 1996 and it was used to build the Mac OS X Operating System and eventually iOS on iPhones and iPads. Objective-C is a thin layer on top of C and retains backward compatibility such that Objective-C compilers can compile C programs.

Software engineering is a team activity. Programming is primarily a solitary activity. Software engineers and computer programmers both develop software applications needed by working computers. The difference between the two positions lies in the responsibilities and the approach to the job. Software engineers use well-defined scientific principles and procedures to deliver an efficient and reliable software product. A software engineer is involved in the complete process. Programming is one aspect of software development. A software engineer works on components with other engineers to build a system. A programmer writes a complete program.

(Total words:1245, taken from:https://www.thoughtco.com/)

New Words and Expressions

off-the-cuff /ˌɔfðəˈkʌf/ adj. with little or no preparation or forethought 即席的

avionics /ˌeviˈɑnɪks/ n. science and technology of electronic systems and devices for aeronautics and astronautics 航空电子设备,航空电子学,航空电子技术

aspiring /əˈspaɪərɪŋ/ adj. desiring or striving for recognition or advancement 有抱负的;追求……的;高耸的

database /ˈdeɪtəbeɪs/ n. an organized body of related information 数据库,资料库

graphical /ˈgræfɪkl/ adj. relating to or presented by a graph; written or drawn or engraved 图解的;绘画的;生动的

manipulation /məˌnɪpjʊˈleɪʃ(ə)n/ n. exerting shrewd or devious influence especially for one's own advantage 操纵

dynamic /daɪˈnæmɪk/ adj. characterized by action or forcefulness or force of personality 动态的,动力的,动力学的

dichotomy /daɪˈkɑtəmɪ/ n. being twofold; a classification into two opposed parts or subclasses 一分成二,对分

compatibility /kəmˌpætɪˈbɪlɪtɪ/ n. capability of existing or performing in harmonious or congenial combination 兼容性

automatically /ɔːtəˈmætɪklɪ/ adv. in a mechanical manner; by a mechanism 自动地；机械地；无意识地

solitary /ˈsɒlɪt(ə)rɪ/ adj. being the only one; single and isolated from others 独自的，独立的

Proper Nouns

SQL　Structured Query Language　结构化查询语言

PHP　Professional Hypertext Preprocessor　服务器端编程语言

XML　eXtensible Markup Language　可扩展标记语言

NASA　National Aeronautics and Space Administration　美国国家航空航天局

Reading Task

Task 1 Use the scanning steps provided at the beginning of the unit to fill in the blanks.

1. Software engineers' job is _____ percent paperwork and _____ percent code.

2. Life-critical systems include aircraft, nuclear reactor controls, and _____ system.

3. Many colleges and universities offer degrees in _____.

4. SQL is the language of _____.

5. Yukihiro Matsumoto designed _____.

6. In 1988, Steve Jobs founded _____ and they licensed Objective-C.

Task 2 Complete the following table about the main points of the text. Use the scanning steps provided at the beginning of the unit.

Software engineer and programmer	Software engineers design and develop computer games, _____, network control systems and _____.
	One distinguishing feature of software engineering is _____ that it produces.
Software engineer and programmer	Programmers write code in one or more of the in-demand programming languages, including: _____, Java, C++, _____, _____, Ruby on Rails, Objective-C, etc..
	Many colleges and universities offer degrees in software engineering. Aspiring software engineers may major in _____, software engineering, _____ or computer information systems.
	Software engineers and computer programmers both develop _____ needed by working computers.
	Software engineering is a _____ activity. Programming is primarily a _____ activity.

Task 3 Decide whether the following statements are true (T) or false (F).

1. Software engineers need strong programming skills to communicate with the programmers and are frequently fluent in several programming languages. (   )

2. Several of the large software companies, including Microsoft, Oracle and Red Hat offer courses toward certifications. (   )

3. All modern relational databases, including Access, FileMaker Pro, Microsoft SQL Server and Oracle use SQL as their basic building block.

( )

4. Like English, Java has a set of numbers that determine how the instructions are written. ( )

5. Modern PCs are fast enough to count to a billion in seconds. ( )

6. Once a program has been written, the high-level instructions are translated into numeric codes that computers can understand and execute. ( )

7. Software engineering is a solitary activity. Programming is primarily a team activity. ( )

8. Objective-C, developed over 30 years ago, was backwards compatible with C but incorporated elements of the programming language Smalltalk. ( )

Task 4 Work in pairs and answer the following questions.

1. "Software engineering treats the approach to developing software as a formal process much like that found in traditional engineering." What does "*the approach*" refer to (Para. 1)?

2. How many programming languages does the author put forward in the passage? And what are they?

3. What is the difference between software engineering and programming? What are the similarities between the software engineers and computer programmers?

Task 5 Group Discussion

Nowadays, software engineering plays an increasingly important role in our society. Many software engineers are working in different walks of life. Work in groups of 3—4 and discuss the following question.

According to Wikipedia, most software engineers and programmers work 40 hours a week, but many work more than 50 hours a week. Potential injuries in these occupations are possible because like other workers who spend long periods sitting in front of a computer terminal typing at a keyboard, engineers and programmers are susceptible to eyestrain, back discomfort, and hand and wrist problems such as carpal tunnel syndrome. What can they do to optimize their work efficiency and at the same time minimize physical injuries?

Language Building-up

Task 1 The following expressions are taken from Text A. Translate the following terms from English into Chinese.

computer programming languages

nuclear power plants

computer operating system

the language of databases

New York Stock Exchange

networking protocols

Task 2 Complete the following sentences with the correct form of the words in the box.

| numeric   dynamic   automatically   solitary |
| aspiring   manipulating   database   compatibility |

1. With the best _____ of networks and OS support, it can be

used in almost every country in the world.

2. She's always borrowing my clothes and _____ me to give her vast sums of money.

3. Many _____ young artists are advised to learn by copying the masters.

4. The swing door will resile _____ after it has been opened.

5. Your job is to group them by letter and put them in _____ order.

6. Paul was a shy, pleasant, _____ man.

7. He's one of the most _____ imaginative jazz pianists of our time.

8. A _____ is a collection of data that is stored in a computer and that can easily be used and added to.

Task 3 Translate the following paragraph into English.

软件工程师是指从事软件职业、具备了工程师资格的人员,包括软件设计人员、软件工程管理人员、程序员等一系列岗位,工作内容都与软件开发生产相关。软件工程师的技术要求是比较全面的,除了最基础的编程语言(C语言/C++/JAVA等)、数据库技术(SQL/ORACLE/DB2等),还有诸多如JAVASCRIPT、AJAX、HIBERNATE、SPRING等前沿技术。软件工程师一般分为四级:软件技术员、助理软件工程师、软件工程师、高级软件工程师。

Passage B Application and System Software

Application software does all the hard work. This type of software performs user related tasks and can further be classified as general purpose, specialist or bespoke. System software tools include OS and utility programs while the software application is task related.

A general purpose application package is a type of software which can undertake different related tasks. Examples of application packages include spreadsheets, databases, word processors, presentation, and graphics software.

Generic System Software Tools: Working Wonders Across Generations

Application software is also referred to as generic software which basically means that it performs the same sort of general tasks as its counterparts. Computer users can purchase applications off the shelf.

Another name for application software is general purpose software. This comprises the following types of application software: Database Packages, Desktop Publishing, Spreadsheet Packages, Word Processing Packages, Graphics Packages, CAD Packages, Communication Software, Presentation Graphics Packages, Web Page Editors, Integrated Packages, Specialist Application Software, etc.

Database packages. Lotus Approach Paradox, MS Access are some of the different database packages which store and retrieve data.

Desktop publishing. These packages such as PageMaker and MS Publisher produce excellent professional publications such as newsletters, books, magazines and more.

Spreadsheet packages include Lotus 123 and MS Excel and are for tasks that involve numerous calculations or productions of graphs or charts.

Word processing packages includes MS Word, WordPerfect and many others which generate text-based documents such as memos, reports, and letters.

Graphics packages. The different types of graphics packages include Corel, Serif Draw, PaintBrush, and Paint. These are used for creating and reshaping artwork.

Computer Applications aided design or CAD Packages such as AutoCAD, TurboCAD, and 2-D Design are excellent for creating and generating architecture plans and engineering designs.

Communication software is used for accessing online email services and websites as well as the internet. The different types of communication software include Mozilla Firefox, Internet Explorer, Netscape Communicator and more.

Presentation graphics packages are excellent for creating professional slide shows and presentations which can be viewed with data or overhead projectors on-screen.

Web page editors such as MSFrontPage, Macromedia and Dreamweaver are used for creating Web pages. Create the perfect page in minutes using these amazing editing tools.

Integrated application packages combine different Apps all in one package offering excellent facilities for graphics, communicating, presenting, word processing and more. Integrated packages also make great savings on cost and applications have lesser number of features as against individual application packages. Microsoft Works is an instance of integrated packages.

Specialist application software performs single specific tasks and examples of such software include payroll management and appointment scheduling.

A Typology That Works: Enterprise Versus Non-Enterprise Application Software

Application software helps end users perform single or numerous tasks. Application software is crucial for work settings too. This forms the basis of the distinction between Enterprise and Non-Enterprise application software.

Enterprise application software includes the following:

• Enterprise resource planning

• Supply chain management

• Embedded software

• CRM/Customer relationship management

Non-Enterprise application software comprises the following:

• Mobile Apps: Application software intended for mobile devices, smartphones or tablets

• Entertainment: Gaming applications for DVD, CD, and media such as Rhapsody and Solitaire

• Graphics: Apps for organizing, editing and sharing images such as Adobe Illustrator, Photosmart Essentials and more

• Security: Detecting firewalls and anti-virus protection programs like QuickHeal and Norton are also perfect for those who want good cyber guards.

• ERP: The Business of Application Software

Among enterprise software, ERP is the most commonly used application. This is the largest application used across the world followed by Office Suites and CRM. ERP integrates all operations and functions while Office Suite is a collection of software programs which can mesh well with each other. Office Suite programs such as MS Office are distributed together.

System software tools provide the platform for running application or application software. It brings together the capabilities of the computer. Tasks that benefit end users fall under the domain of application software. ERP and supply chain management includes applications for services and manufacturing.

CRM or customer relationship management is a part of the enterprise software market for providing functionality to an enterprise in sales, marketing, customer service, and support.

Application software aids end users to perform single or multiple tasks and has enterprise as well as nonenterprise versions. It is used to design and accomplish specific tasks such as playing video files, editing images or composing a letter. The software program, as well as its implementation and the capabilities and power of the computer platform, encompasses systems software.

Systems programs differ from application programs. One of the unique characteristics of an application software program is the prevalence of user interface that is graphical in nature or GUI/Graphical User Interface. Such programs offer end users creativity to compose user-written software as well for word processing, accounting, and filtering data. Text editing is one of the many different types of application software that allows the development of more software programs and serves as a base. Web developers can use text editors to code client and server-side scripts for increased functionality of web pages.

A text editor is, in other words, an application software designed to create a script which is an application in itself. When application programs are bundled together, this is referred to as application suite. Application software suites include everything from a word processor to spreadsheets, image manipulation and drawing. From embedding spreadsheets into word processor created documents to inserting edited images, the possibilities are endless. While application software manipulates data or text for providing information, systems programs are involved in manipulation of computer hardware resources. System software forms the basis on which application software operates.

Application Software: Program + Implementation

Application software is conceived of as software along with its implementation. From accounting software to media players, the areas of application are tremendous. An application software is like a microchip in the computer hardware. It is part of a whole. System software tools help in operating the hardware and provide a base for running the application software. Application software executes in an environment created by system software tools. System software tools itself executes within an environment that is self-created. System software tools require complex programming, while application software requires a simpler version. Many more different types of application software are there compared to system software programs. While system software programs run in the background, application software runs in the foreground and users interact with it. System software programs work on its own while application software is dependent on it. Both work together allowing the computer to function as a whole.

System software programs are widely used as general purpose software, have common tasks and special purpose applications are narrower in their approach and associated with specific tasks. Another categorization of application software is horizontal or vertical. While horizontal programs are for generalized use with consumers, vertical programs are designed for the purpose of specialized uses. Horizontal Apps include multimedia and graphics, internet programs and more. Copyrighted software includes shareware and commercial programs as well as freeware. To use a computer with skill and efficiency, mastery of application software is a must.

Conclusion

Application software is as important to the functioning of a computer as its hardware. Application software, in its wide and varied avatars, is the perfect tool for utilizing the computer well. This type of software is distinct from a system or operational software, yet it is linked to them as well.

Computing involves the use of interrelated software to do all the hard tasks. Application software is an integral part of computing.

(Total words:1260 ,taken from:https://www. educba. com/)

New Words and Expressions

bespoke /bɪˈspəʊk/ adj. of clothing (esp. of clothing or a website, computer program, etc.) made to the customer's specifications 订制的

utility /juːˈtɪlɪtɪ/ n. an important service such as water, electricity, or gas that is provided for everyone, and that everyone pays for 实用,公用设施

spreadsheets /ˈspredʃiːts/ n. a computer program that is used for displaying and dealing with numbers 电子表格,电子数据表

graphics /ˈɡræfɪks/ n. the process or art of drawing in accordance with mathematical principles 制图法

counterpart /ˈkaʊntəpɑːrt/ n. another person or thing that has a similar function or position in a different place 对应的人或物

desktop /ˈdesktɒp/ n. a convenient size for using on a desk or table, but are not designed to be portable 台式电脑

Lotus /ˈləʊtəs/ n. a type of water lily that grows in Africa and Asia 莲花(汽车品牌)

payroll /ˈpeɪrəʊl/ n. a list of employees and their salaries, the department that determines the amounts of wage or salary due to each employee 工资名单;在册职工人数

domain /də(ʊ)ˈmeɪn/ n. a particular field of thought, activity, or interest, especially one over which someone has control, influence, or rights; a set of addresses that shows, for example, the category or geographical area that an Internet address belongs to 领域;域名

implementation /ˌɪmplɪmenˈteɪʃ(ə)n/ n. the act of accomplishing some aim or executing some order; the act of implementing (providing a practical means for accomplishing something); carrying into effect 成就;实现;履行;安装启用

filtering /ˈfɪltərɪŋ/ v. pass a substance through a device which is designed to remove certain particles contained in it 过滤

embed /ɪmˈbed/ v. fix or set securely or deeply; attach to, as a journalist to a military unit when reporting on a war 植入;把……嵌入;派遣(战地记者等)

microchip /ˈmaɪkrə(ʊ)tʃɪp/ n. electronic equipment consisting of a small crystal of a silicon semiconductor fabricated to carry out a number of electronic functions in an integrated circuit 微型集成电路片,微晶片

foreground /ˈfɔːgraʊnd/ n. the part of a scene that is near the viewer;(computer science) a window for an active application 前景;最显著的位置

horizontal /ˌhɒrɪˈzɒnt(ə)l/ n. something that is oriented horizontally 水平线,水平面,水平位置;adj. parallel to or in the plane of the horizon or a baseline 水平的;地平线的;同一阶层

vertical /ˈvɜːtɪk(ə)l/ n. something that is oriented vertically 垂直线,垂直面;adj. at right angles to the plane of the horizon or a base line 垂直的,直立的

multimedia /ˈmʌltɪmiːdɪə/ n. transmission that combine media of communication (text and graphics and sound etc.) 多媒体

copyright /ˈkɒpɪraɪt/ n. a document granting exclusive right to publish and sell literary or musical or artistic work 版权,著作权 v. secure a copyright on a written work 保护版权;为……取得版权

avatar /ˈævətɑː/ n. a new personification of a familiar idea 化身

paintbrush /ˈpeɪntbrʌʃ/ n. a brush used as an applicator (to apply paint) 漆画

Proper Nouns

OS   Operating System   操作系统

CAD   Computer-Aided Design   计算机辅助设计

CRM   Customer Relationship Management   客户关系管理

ERP   Enterprise Resource Planning   企业资源计划

GUI   Graphical User Interface   图形用户界面

Corel   科立尔(加拿大一家软件公司名)

Netscape   美国网景公司,以开发浏览器闻名

Reading Task

Task 1 Use the scanning steps provided at the beginning of the unit to fill in the blanks.

1. Another name for application software is _____ software.

2. MS Excel belongs to _____; MS Word belongs to _____; Paintbrush belongs to _____; AutoCAD belongs to _____; Mozilla Firefox belongs to _____.

3. _____ are excellent for creating professional slide shows and presentations which can be viewed with data or overhead projectors on-screen.

4. Microsoft works is an instance of _____.

5. Such tasks as payroll management and appointment scheduling are performed by _____.

Task 2 Use the scanning steps provided at the beginning of the unit to fill in the table.

		System Software	Application Software
Differences		Help in operating the _____ and provide base for running _____.	Execute in an environment created by _____.
		Require _____ programming.	Require _____ programming.
		Run in the _____	Run in the _____
		Work on its own.	_____
Similarity		Work together allowing the computer to function as a whole.	

Task 3 Work in pairs and answer the following questions. Identify the part of the text that supports your answer.

1. What does enterprise application software include?

2. What does non-enterprise application software include?

3. What features do ERP and CRM have?

4. What is application suite?

Language Building-up

Task 1 Translate the following sentences from the passage into Chinese.

1. Examples of application packages include spreadsheets, databases, word processors, presentation, and graphics software.

_____

_____

2. CRM or customer relationship management is a part of the enterprise software market for providing functionality to an enterprise in sales, marketing, customer service, and support.

_____

_____

3. One of the unique characteristics of an application software program is the prevalence of user interface that is graphical in nature or GUI/Graphical User Interface.

_____

_____

4. System software programs are widely used as general purpose software, have common tasks and special purpose applications are more narrow in their approach and associated with specific tasks.

_____

_____

5. While application software manipulates data or text for providing information, systems programs are involved in manipulation of computer

hardware resources.

Task 2 The following expressions are taken from Passage B. Translate the following terms from English into Chinese.

enterprise resource planning

supply chain management

embedded software

user-written software

cyber guards

Task 3 Paraphrase the following sentences from the passage.

1. A general purpose application package is a type of software which can undertake different related tasks.

2. This forms the basis of the distinction between Enterprise and Non-Enterprise application software.

3. Application software, in its wide and varied avatars, is the perfect tool for utilizing the computer well.

4. Application software is conceived of as software along with its

implementation.

5. Horizontal Apps include multimedia and graphics, internet programs and more. Copyrighted software includes shareware and commercial programs as well as freeware.

Part Three Academic Writing

Theme-related Writing

On the basis of what you have learned from this unit, write an essay entitled "Software Engineering and Its Application". You should write at least 150 words but no more than 200 words.

Unit 3 Internet

Part One Academic Reading Skills

Predicting

Predicting is a strategy in reading comprehension that readers use to anticipate what comes next based on clues from the text and by using their prior knowledge.

Effective readers use titles, headings, pictures, and texts, as well as personal experiences to make predictions before they begin to read. Predicting involves thinking ahead while reading and anticipating information and events in the text. After making predictions, students can read through the text and refine, revise, and verify their predictions. The strategy of making predictions actively engages students and connects them to the text by asking them what they think might occur in the reading.

The methods of predicting can be listed as follows:

1. Before-reading Prediction

1) Use the skill of skimming to predict the information in the text;

2) Use knowledge of the subject matter to predict about content;

2. While-reading Prediction

Using prior knowledge of the subject and the ideas in the text to

1) predict about the meanings of unknown words;

2) predict about the idea of the following sentences and paragraphs;

3) predict about the text type and writing style;

Part Two Passage Reading

Passage A What Is Internet?

Pre-reading Task

Directions: *Read the title and discuss the following questions in groups.*

1. Do you know when the original conceptual foundation of the Internet was proposed?

2. What do you usually do with the Internet? What function do you apply most frequently?

Life today is highly dependent on computers—they do most of the important work and are found everywhere—from homes to police stations, government institutions and military facilities. However, the computer would have never been so popular and widely spread if it was not for the Internet.

History

When the original conceptual foundation of the Internet was laid back in the 1950s, no one had the slightest idea of how far this project would go. At those insecure post-war times of alienation and deepening political division, the vision of the Internet as we see it today, was only a matter of science fiction dreaming. Starting as a military project in the United States, it quickly became very popular in several other countries.

Now, several decades later, with the spread of the democratic lifestyle and the amazing technological progress, we all witness the existence of a parallel world of unlimited communication possibilities that occupies an increasing part of our daily routine with the sole purpose of facilitating our lives.

The Internet Today—Common Uses

The dynamic, user-friendly interface of the Internet as we know it today, is breathed life into by a multi-layer global network system that connects hundreds of millions of computers. This large system is comprised of multiple local and global networks serving private, public, business, academic and government purposes, which allows for the exchange of data between more than a hundred Internet-linked countries worldwide. This makes the Internet an enormous carrier of various information resources and services, such as text and multi-media data, email, online chat, VoIP, file transfer and file sharing, ecommerce, online gaming, etc.

The Email

The Email is probably one of the most popular features, which came alongside with the creation of the Internet. Today, almost every person on the planet has an email address somewhere, be it a self hosted email address or an email address with some of the free email providers, such as Google or Yahoo. The Email, which was originally intended to act as an alternative to letters, today represents so much more, making the communication between people on different sides of the planet very easy. Today, there are even enterprises, which handle their entire online business, relying solely on email based communication.

At NTC Hosting you can find a powerful email solution coming with several features, such as an email auto-responder, which can be used to send an automated reply to every message sent to you; an anti-spam filter, via which you can stop unwanted emails; an anti-virus protection service, which checks all your emails for viruses; and an email forwarding function, through which you can forward all your emails to one mailbox. With NTC Hosting you can also create mailing lists for your hosted emails, which can send one single email message to several subscribers simultaneously.

E-commerce

With the growth of the Internet and the number of its users, a huge market share was created. Before, to hold an enterprise you had to have an office and cover all kinds of additional expenses, whereas now you can just create a website with one of the several e-commerce script solutions, and have your own online shop in a matter of minutes.

This has allowed a lot of small businesses to grow, making their products available worldwide to a much wider audience.

With all web hosting plans offered by NTC Hosting, our users can have an e-commerce solution pre-installed and readily available. You can have one easily installed in your account at any time with the help of our popular PHP Scripts Installer.

File Transfer and Sharing

The transfer of files over the Internet has existed since the creation of the latter. Today, with the majority of information being stored on files, their safe transfer and sharing has become a big necessity. A popular way to transfer files is to send them via email as attachments. This, however, is not the best way, since several providers place restrictions on the type of files that can be sent, or on their size. This is why the File Transfer Protocol was created. It allows a user running an FTP program to connect to an FTP-enabled server and safely transfer files to this server. Once they are on the server, they can be downloaded by everyone.

There are a lot of Free FTP software solutions, which allow you to seamlessly connect and transfer files. With all NTC Hosting plans, users can take advantage of our powerful FTP solution. With each of our CMS hosting and Low-Cost hosting offers, you can take advantage of numerous FTP accounts, making FTP transfer and sharing a breeze.

The Nature of the Internet

The explosive growth of the Internet over the last decade is attributed to two basic reasons—the non-centralized management of its development and the non-proprietary nature of its main functional units—the Internet protocols. This "freedom" of the Internet determines its balanced organic growth and prevents it from suffering the consequences of monopoly. The only Internet-related entity with central coordinating functions is ICANN, which controls the assignment of domain names and IP addresses on a global scale—a very necessary role that works for the organized distribution of unique website names to users worldwide.

Internet Access

Since browsing the Internet is considered as a pretty normal daily activity such as picking up the phone to make a phone call, for example, the Internet access points have become an indelible part of the communication infrastructure today. Public Internet-connected places include libraries, airports, coffee shops, hotels, and specialized Internet cafes. Thanks to the Wi-Fi technology, the Internet can now be accessed by every laptop/PDA equipped person within wireless-connection enabled areas such as campuses, malls, parks and even entire cities. The mobile phone industry has also been affected by the Internet with almost every newly released phone model offering access to the global network.

Internet / WWW Disambiguation

Talking about the Internet, it is important to point out that it is not identical in meaning with the World Wide Web. Both terms are increasingly used as synonyms on a global scale, although this is not correct from a technical point of view. The reason for this common misunderstanding is that the World Wide Web is the most popular Internet application today. Anyway, you should distinguish both terms, knowing that the World Wide Web represents the huge set of interlinked text documents, images and other resources presented on the websites and linked by means of hyperlinks and URL elements, while the Internet provides the physical environment for the web to exist.

(Total words: 1098, taken from https://www.ntchosting.com/encyclopedia/internet/what-is-internet/)

New Words and Expressions

institution /ˌɪnstɪˈtjuːʃn/ n. a large important organization that has a particular purpose, for example, a university or bank(大学、银行等规模大的)机构

facility /fəˈsɪləti/ n. buildings, services, equipment, etc. that are provided for a particular purpose 设施

conceptual /kənˈseptʃuəl/ adj. (formal) related to or based on ideas 概念(上)的,观念(上)的

alienation /ˌeɪliəˈneɪʃn/ n. the action to cause people to be emotionally or intellectually separated from 异化,疏远

democratic /ˌdeməˈkrætɪk/ adj. controlled by representatives who are elected by the people of a country 民主的,民主政体的

parallel /ˈpærəlel/ adj. Two or more lines that are parallel to each other are the same distance apart at every point. 平行的

interface /ˈɪntəfeɪs/ n. (computing) the way a computer program presents information to a user or receives information from a user, in particular the layout of the screen and the menus (计)(人机)界面

anti-spam /ˈæntispæm/n. (computing) the action to prevent people or organizations from sending unwanted e-mails, usually as advertising 反垃圾信息;反垃圾邮件

subscriber /səbˈskraɪbə/n. a person who pays to receive a service 消费者,用户

simultaneously /ˌsɪməlˈteɪniəsli/ adv. happening or existing at the same time 同时发生地,同时出现地

restriction /rɪˈstrɪkʃn/ n. a rule or law that limits what you can do or what can happen 限制,约束

seamlessly /ˈsiːmləsli/ adv. with no spaces or pauses between one part and the next 天衣无缝地,无缝地

non-proprietary /ˌnɑːnprəˈpraɪəteri/ adj. not made by or belonging to a particular 无产权的;非专属的;非专利的

monopoly /məˈnɒpəli/ n. (business) the complete control of trade in particular goods or the supply of a particular service; a type of goods or a service that is controlled in this way (商)垄断;专营服务;被垄断的商品(或服务)

indelible /ɪnˈdeləbl/ adj. impossible to forget or remove 无法忘记的;不可磨灭的

infrastructure /ˈɪnfrəstrʌktʃə/ n. the basic systems and services that are necessary for a country or an organization to run smoothly(国家或机构的)基础设施,基础建设

identical /aɪˈdentɪkl/ adj. similar in every detail 完全同样的,相同的

synonym /ˈsɪnənɪm/ n. a word or expression that has the same or nearly the same meaning as another in the same language 同义词

hyperlink /ˈhaɪpərlɪŋk/ n. a place in an electronic document on a computer that is linked to another electronic document 超级链接,超链接

disambiguation /ˌdɪsæmbɪɡjʊˈeɪʃən/ n. clarification that follows from the removal of ambiguity 消除歧义,解疑

Proper Nouns

NTC Hosting　知名的主机服务公司,可提供功能强大和种类繁多的托管服务

FTP program　文件传送协议程序

CMS　Content Management System　内容管理系统

ICANN　The Internet Corporation for Assigned Names and Numbers　互联网名称与数字地址分配机构,对互联网唯一标识符系统及其安全稳定的运营进行协调

PDA　Personal Digital Assistant　掌上电脑,个人数字助理

Wi-Fi　wireless fidelity　无线局域网,无线网络

WWW　World Wide Web　环球信息网,也称"万维网","环球网"

URL　Uniform Resource Locator　统一资源定位符

Reading Task

Task 1 Predict Passage A according to the following questions.

1. Look at the title *Internet* and predict the main contents of the passage.

2. Skim the subtitles and predict the major details of the passage.

3. Share your predictions with your partners and find the similarities and discrepancies.

Task 2 Predict the meanings of italicized words and phrases of the following sentences.

1. This makes the Internet an *enormous carrier* of various information resources and services, such as text and multi-media data, email, online chat, VoIP, file transfer and file sharing, ecommerce, online gaming, etc.

2. At NTC Hosting you can find a powerful email solution coming with several features, such as an email *auto-responder*, which can be used to send an automated reply to every message sent to you...

3. The only Internet-related entity with central coordinating functions is ICANN, which controls the assignment of domain names and IP addresses on a global scale—a very necessary role that works for the organized *distribution* of unique website names to users worldwide.

Task 3 Complete the following table about the main points of the text.

File transfer and sharing	1. Today, the information whose ____ and ____ has been necessary.
	2. A popular way to transfer files is to ____.
	3. ____ is why the File Transfer Protocol was created.
	4. Files are ____, so they can be downloaded by everyone.

59

Task 4 Decide whether the following statements are true (T) or false (F).

1. The explosive growth of the Internet over the last decade includes three basic reasons. (   )

2. The only Internet-related entity with central coordinating functions is CMS. (   )

3. The Internet can be accessed within wireless-connection enabled areas because of the Wi-Fi technology. (   )

4. Now every mobile phone offers access to the global network. (   )

Task 5 Work in pairs and answer the following questions.

1. What was the vision of the Internet like at the chaotic post-war times?

2. Nowadays, the Internet has become one of the most common carriers in our daily life. Hence, what kinds of information resources and services can the Internet provide according to the text?

3. How is an on-line shop at present different from the traditional establishment of an enterprise in the past, thanks to the development of the Internet?

4. How could you demonstrate the differences between the Internet and the World Wide Web?

Task 6 Group Discussion

Nowadays, the Internet has an effect on most aspects of our life. Some think that it brings positive influence while others think that there are some negative factors about Internet. Please talk about it with your partners and present your opinions.

Language Building-up

Task 1 The following expressions are taken from Text A. Translate the following terms from English into Chinese.

original conceptual foundation

insecure post-war times

daily routine

file transfer and sharing

on a global scale

offer access to

Task 2 Match each word with the best definition.

parallel	not made by or belonging to a particular
restriction	the complete control of trade in particular goods or service
seamlessly	with no spaces or pauses between one part and the next
non-proprietary	the same distance apart at every point
monopoly	basic systems and services that are necessary for a country
indelible	impossible to forget or remove
infrastructure	a rule or law that limits what you can do or what can happen

Task 3 Complete the following sentences with the correct form of the words in the box.

| institution   conceptual   alienation |
| democratic   identical   disambiguation |

1. She then explained some of the _____ knowledge and hoped the students would understand her introduction.

2. The _____ treatment of such different items is totally illogical.

3. They will be able to choose their own leaders in _____ elections.

4. If the original author wrote in Thai without _____, our searching would be not that much difficult.

5. The government built a charitable _____ for the education of young children.

6. Ecological crisis is the _____ of both the relationship between man and nature and that between man and man.

Task 4 Translate the following paragraph into English.

5G 网络的产生对世界网络的影响非常之大，我们现在使用 4G 有时会觉得网速缓慢，让我们从事工作或学习娱乐都不方便。5G 的最大优势就是可以快速地连接网络，并在几秒钟内实现下载等。它还可以比较灵活地支持各种不同的机器设备。4G 网络大多数就是支持手机和电脑；但是我们生活的这个时代已经进入了智能化时代，每一种家电、智能化工具、科学技术研究设备都需要网络来连接。所以当我们进入 5G 时代，这一些设备就可以进入互联网,实现真正的智能化。

Passage B Computer Network

Internet, a system architecture that has revolutionized communications and methods of commerce by allowing various computer networks around the world to interconnect. Sometimes referred to as a "network of networks", the Internet emerged in the United States in the 1970s but did not become visible to the general public until the early 1990s. By 2015, approximately 3.2 billion people, or nearly half of the world's population, were estimated to have access to the Internet.

The Internet provides a capability so powerful and general that it can be used for almost any purpose that depends on information, and it is accessible by every individual who connects to one of its constituent networks. It supports human communication via electronic mail (e-mail), "chat rooms", newsgroups, and audio and video transmission and allows people to work collaboratively at many different locations. It supports access to digital information by many applications, including the World Wide Web. The Internet has proved to be a spawning ground for a large and growing number of "e-businesses" (including subsidiaries of traditional "brick-and-mortar" companies) that carry out most of their sales and services over the Internet. Many experts believe that the Internet will dramatically transform business as well as society.

Origin and Development of Early Networks

The first computer networks were dedicated special-purpose systems such as SABRE (an airline reservation system) and AUTODIN I (a defense command-and-control system), both designed and implemented in the late 1950s and early 1960s. By the early 1960s computer manufacturers had begun to use semiconductor technology in commercial products, and both conventional batch-processing and time-sharing systems were in place in many large, technologically advanced companies. Time-sharing systems allowed a computer's resources to be shared in rapid succession with multiple users, cycling through the queue of users so quickly that the computer appeared dedicated to each user's tasks despite the existence of many others accessing the system "simultaneously". This led to the notion of sharing computer resources (called host computers or simply hosts) over an entire network. Host-to-host interactions were envisioned, along with access to specialized resources (such as supercomputers and mass storage systems) and interactive access by remote users to the computational powers of time-sharing systems located elsewhere. These ideas were first realized in ARPANET, which established the first host-to-host network connection on Oct. 29, 1969. It was created by the Advanced Research Projects Agency (ARPA) of the U. S. Department of Defense. ARPANET was one of the first general-purpose computer networks. It connected time-sharing computers at government-supported research sites, principally universities in the United States, and it soon became a critical piece of infrastructure for the computer science research community in the United States. Tools and applications—such as the simple mail transfer protocol

(SMTP, commonly referred to as e-mail), for sending short messages, and the file transfer protocol (FTP), for longer transmissions—quickly emerged. In order to achieve cost-effective interactive communications between computers, which typically communicate in short bursts of data, ARPANET employed the new technology of packet switching. Packet switching takes large messages (or chunks of computer data) and breaks them into smaller, manageable pieces (known as packets) that can travel independently over any available circuit to the target destination, where the pieces are reassembled. Thus, unlike traditional voice communications, packet switching does not require a single dedicated circuit between each pair of users.

Commercial packet networks were introduced in the 1970s, but these were designed principally to provide efficient access to remote computers by dedicated terminals. Briefly, they replaced long-distance modem connections by less-expensive "virtual" circuits over packet networks. In the United States, Telenet and Tymnet were two such packet networks. Neither supported host-to-host communications; in the 1970s this was still the province of the research networks, and it would remain so for many years.

DARPA (Defense Advanced Research Projects Agency; formerly ARPA) supported initiatives for ground-based and satellite-based packet networks. The ground-based packet radio system provided mobile access to computing resources, while the packet satellite network connected the United States with several European countries and enabled connections with widely dispersed and remote regions. With the introduction of packet radio, connecting a mobile terminal to a computer network became feasible. However, time-sharing systems were then still too large, unwieldy, and costly to be mobile or even to exist outside a climate-controlled computing environment. A strong motivation thus existed to connect the packet radio network to ARPANET in order to allow mobile users with simple terminals to access the time-sharing systems for which they had authorization. Similarly, the packet satellite network was used by DARPA to link the United States with satellite terminals serving the United Kingdom, Norway, Germany, and Italy. These terminals, however, had to be connected to other networks in European countries in order to reach the end users. Thus arose the need to connect the packet satellite net, as well as the packet radio net, with other networks.

Foundation of the Internet

The Internet resulted from the effort to connect various research networks in the United States and Europe. First, DARPA established a program to investigate the interconnection of "heterogeneous networks". This program, called Internetting, was based on the newly introduced concept of open architecture networking, in which networks with defined standard interfaces would be interconnected by "gateways". A working demonstration of the concept was planned. In order for the concept to work, a new protocol had to be designed and developed; indeed, a system architecture was also required.

In 1974 Vinton Cerf, then at Stanford University in California, and this author, then at DARPA, collaborated on a paper that first described such a protocol and system architecture—namely, the transmission control protocol (TCP), which enabled different types of machines on networks all over the world to route and assemble data packets. TCP, which originally included the Internet protocol (IP), a global addressing mechanism that allowed routers to get data packets to their ultimate destination, formed the TCP/IP standard, which was adopted by the U. S. Department of Defense in 1980. By the early 1980s the "open architecture" of the TCP/IP approach was adopted and endorsed by many other researchers and eventually by technologists and businessmen around the world.

By the 1980s other U. S. governmental bodies were heavily involved with networking, including the National Science Foundation (NSF), the Department of Energy, and the National Aeronautics and Space Administration (NASA). While DARPA had played a seminal role in creating a small-scale version of the Internet among its researchers, NSF worked with DARPA to expand access to the entire scientific and academic community and to make TCP/IP the standard in all federally supported research networks. In 1985—1986 NSF funded the first five supercomputing centres—at Princeton University, the University of Pittsburgh, the University of California, San Diego, the University of Illinois, and Cornell University. In the 1980s NSF also funded the development and operation of the NSFNET, a national "backbone" network to connect these centres. By the late 1980s the network was operating at millions of bits per second. NSF also funded various nonprofit local and regional networks to connect other users to the NSFNET. A few commercial networks also began in the late 1980s; these were soon joined by others, and the Commercial Internet eXchange (CIX) was formed to allow transit traffic between commercial networks that otherwise would not have been allowed on the NSFNET backbone. In 1995, after extensive review of the situation, NSF decided that support of the NSFNET infrastructure was no longer required, since many commercial providers were now willing and able to meet the needs of the research community, and its support was withdrawn. Meanwhile, NSF had fostered a competitive collection of commercial Internet backbones connected to one another through so-called network access points (NAPs).

From the Internet's origin in the early 1970s, control of it steadily devolved from government stewardship to private-sector participation and finally to private custody with government oversight and forbearance. Today a loosely structured group of several thousand interested individuals known as the Internet Engineering Task Force participates in a grassroots development process for Internet standards. Internet standards are maintained by the nonprofit Internet Society, an international body with headquarters in Reston, Virginia. The Internet Corporation for Assigned Names and Numbers (ICANN), another nonprofit, private organization, oversees various aspects of policy regarding Internet domain names and numbers.

Commercial Expansion

The rise of commercial Internet services and applications helped to fuel a rapid commercialization of the Internet. This phenomenon was the result of several other factors as well. One important factor was the introduction of the personal computer and the workstation in the early 1980s—a development that in turn was fueled by unprecedented progress in integrated circuit technology and an attendant rapid decline in computer prices. Another factor, which took on increasing importance, was the emergence of ethernet and other "local area networks" to link personal computers. But other forces were at work too. Following the restructuring of AT&T in 1984, NSF took advantage of various new options for national-level digital backbone services for the NSFNET. In 1988 the Corporation for National Research Initiatives received approval to conduct an experiment linking a commercial e-mail service (MCI Mail) to the Internet. This application was the first Internet connection to a commercial provider that was not also part of the research community. Approval quickly followed to allow other e-mail providers access, and the Internet began its first explosion in traffic.

(Total words: 1595, taken from: https://www.britannica.com/technology/Internet)

New Words and Expressions

revolutionize /ˌrevəˈluːʃənaɪz/ v. to completely change the way that sth. is done 彻底改变,完全变革

approximately /əˈprɒksɪmətli/ adv. used to show that sth. is almost, but not completely, accurate or correct 大概,大约

accessible /əkˈsesəbl/ adj. that can be reached, entered, used, seen, etc. 可到达的,可接近的,可进入的

collaboratively /kəˈlæbəreɪtɪvli/ adv. (formal) involving, or done by, several people or groups of people working together 合作地,协作地,协力地

spawn /spɔːn/ v. to cause sth. to develop or be produced 引发,引起,导致,造成

semiconductor /ˌsemikənˈdʌktə/ n. a solid substance that conducts electricity in particular conditions, better than insulators but not as well as conductors 半导体

succession /səkˈseʃn/ n. a number of people or things that follow each other in time or order 一连串,一系列,连续的人(或事物)

envision /ɪnˈvɪʒn/ v. to imagine what a situation will be like in the future, especially a situation you intend to work towards 展望;想象

reassemble /ˌriːəˈsembl/ v. to fit the parts of sth. together again after it has been taken apart 重新装配(或组装)

initiative /ɪˈnɪʃətɪv/ n. the ability to decide and act on your own without waiting for sb. to tell you what to do 主动性,积极性,自发性

dispersed /dɪˈspɜːst/ adj. Things that are dispersed are situated in many different places, a long way apart from each other. 分散的,散布的

terminal /ˈtɜːmɪnl/ n. a piece of equipment, usually consisting of a keyboard and a screen that joins the user to a central computer system 终端;终端机

mechanism /ˈmekənɪzəm/ n. a special way of getting something done within a particular system 方法;途径;程序;机制

unprecedented /ʌnˈpresɪdentɪd/ adj. that has never happened, been done or been known before 前所未有的,空前的,没有先例的

Proper Nouns

brick-and-mortar   also bricks and mortar or B&M   实体

ARPA   Advanced Research Project Agency   "阿帕",美国高级研究计划署的简称

DARPA   Defense Advanced Research Projects Agency   美国国防高级研究计划局

TCP   Transmission Control Protocol   传输控制协议

NSF   National Science Foundation, United States   美国国家科学基金会

CIX   Commercial Internet Exchange   商务因特网交换中心

AT&T   American Telephone & Telegraph   美国电话电报公司

MCI   Media Control Interface   媒体控制接口

Reading Task

Task 1 Predict Passage B according to the following questions.

1. Look at the title *COMPUTER NETWORK* and predict the main contents of the passage.

2. Skim the subtitles and predict the major details of the passage.

3. Share your predictions with your partners and find the similarities and discrepancies.

Task 2 Predict the meanings of italicized words and phrases of the following sentences.

1. By the early 1960s computer manufacturers had begun to use semiconductor technology in commercial products, and both *conventional batch-processing* and time-sharing systems were in place in many large, technologically advanced companies.

2. A strong motivation thus existed to connect the packet radio network to ARPANET in order to allow mobile users with simple terminals to access the time-sharing systems for which they had *authorization*.

3. Today a loosely structured group of several thousand interested individuals known as the Internet Engineering Task Force participates in a *grassroots* development process for Internet standards.

Task 3 Work in pairs and answer the following questions.

1. What technology was used in commercial products?

2. Why did ARPANET employ the new technology of packet switching?

3. When did a few commercial networks begin?

4. What factors fueled the commercial expansion of the Internet?

Language Building-up

Task 1 Translate the following sentences from the passage into Chinese.

1. The Internet provides a capability so powerful and general that it can be used for almost any purpose that depends on information.

2. Many experts believe that the Internet will dramatically transform business as well as society.

3. The rise of commercial Internet services and applications helped to fuel a rapid commercialization of the Internet.

4. This application was the first Internet connection to a commercial provider that was not also part of the research community.

Task 2 Paraphrase the following sentences from the passage.

1. The Internet is accessible by every individual who connects to one of its constituent networks.

2. With the introduction of packet radio, connecting a mobile terminal to a computer network became feasible.

_____

_____

3. In order to achieve cost-effective interactive communications between computers, which typically communicate in short bursts of data, ARPANET employed the new technology of packet switching.

_____

_____

4. From the Internet's origin in the early 1970s, control of it steadily devolved from government stewardship to private-sector participation and finally to private custody with government oversight and forbearance.

_____

_____

Part Three Academic Writing

Theme-related Writing

On the basis of what you have learned from this unit, write an essay entitled "How does Internet change my life?". You should write at least 150 words but no more than 200 words.

Unit 4 Electronic Business

Part One Academic Reading Skills

Inferring

When the meanings of words are not stated clearly in the context of the text, they may be implied, that is, suggested or hinted at. When meanings are implied, you may infer them.

When you infer, you go beyond the surface details to see other meanings that the details suggest or imply. Successful inferences can be achieved by:

1. Perceiving the detailed description of an event, and sometimes the organization of the passage: the introduction, development and conclusion;

2. Trying to evoke in mind what prior knowledge you have, and sometimes understand the reasoning and logic of the author;

3. Relating the ideas and deducing additional meaning from them.

Part Two Passage Reading

Passage A Ecommerce

Pre-reading Task

Directions: *Read the title and discuss the following questions in groups.*

1. Do you often shop online? Why?

2. What do you know about ecommerce? What advantages are there about ecommerce?

What Is Ecommerce?

Essentially, ecommerce (or electronic commerce) is the buying and selling of goods (or services) on the Internet. From mobile shopping to online payment encryption and beyond, ecommerce encompasses a wide variety of data, systems, and tools for both online buyers and sellers. Most businesses with an ecommerce presence use an ecommerce store and/or an ecommerce platform to conduct both online marketing and sales activities and to oversee logistics and fulfillment. Keep in mind that ecommerce has a few different spelling variations. All of these are synonymous and correct—their use is largely preference-based.

Types of Ecommerce

Generally, there are six main models of ecommerce that businesses can be categorized into:

1. Business-to-Consumer (B2C).

B2C ecommerce ecompasses transactions made between a business and a consumer. This is one of the most widely used sales models in the ecommerce context. When you buy shoes from an online shoe retailer, it is a business-to-consumer transaction.

2. Business-to-Business (B2B).

B2B ecommerce relates to sales made between businesses, such as a manufacturer and a wholesaler or retailer. This type of ecommerce is not consumer-facing and happens only between business entities. Most often, business-to-business sales focus on raw materials or products that are repackaged or combined before being sold to customers.

3. Consumer-to-Consumer (C2C).

One of the earliest forms of ecommerce is the C2C ecommerce business model. Customer-to-customer relates to the sale of products or services between, you guessed it: customers. This would include customer to customer selling relationships like those seen on eBay or Amazon, for example.

4. Consumer-to-Business (C2B).

C2B reverses the traditional ecommerce model (and is what we commonly see in crowdfunding projects). C2B means individual consumers make their products or services available for business buyers. An example of this would be a business model like iStockPhoto, in which stock photos are available online for purchase directly from different photographers.

5. Business-to-Administration (B2A).

This model covers the transactions made between online businesses and administrations. An example would be the products and services related to legal documents, social security, etc.

6. Consumer-to-Administration (C2A).

Same idea here, but with consumers selling online products or services to an administration. C2A might include things like online consulting for education, online tax preparation, etc. Both B2A and C2A are focused around increased efficiency within the government via the support of information technology.

The Impact of Ecommerce

The impact of ecommerce is far and wide with a ripple effect on everything from small business to global enterprise and beyond.

1. Large retailers are forced to sell online.

For many retailers, the growth of ecommerce has expanded their brands' reach and has positively impacted their bottom lines. But for other retailers who have been slow to embrace the online marketplace, the impact has been felt differently. At a high level, retailers that fall into the middle ground are the ones feeling the biggest changes in response to the impact of ecommerce. Foursquare data shows discount stores and luxury retailers are maintaining their footholds with consumers, but ecommerce adds to the fierce competition for retailers within the mid-tier. Research also indicates that one type of retailer in particular has seen a major impact from the rise of ecommerce: department stores. As Amazon becomes consumers' go-to source for products traditionally purchased at department stores, chains like Sears and Macy's (for example) have seen decreased sales across the board.

2. Ecommerce helps small businesses sell directly to customers.

For many small businesses, ecommerce adoption has been a slow process. However, those who've embraced it have discovered ecommerce can open doors to new opportunities that were never possible before. Slowly, small business owners are launching ecommerce stores and diversifying their offerings, reaching more customers, and better accommodating customers who prefer online/mobile shopping. Gallup research shows that 2 in 10 small businesses have expanded their ecommerce presence over the last two years, and 11% say they plan to increase their ecommerce efforts in the coming year.

3. B2B companies start offering B2C-like online ordering experiences.

Data from Four51 indicates that in the B2B world, ecommerce will account for the majority of sales by as soon as 2020—while other data sets show that 79% if B2B customers already expect to be able to place orders from an ecommerce website.

Ecommerce solutions enable self-service, provide more user-friendly platforms for price comparison, and help B2B brands better maintain relationships with buyers, too. What's more, scholarly research indicates ecommerce has made a large positive impact in the B2B market by enabling process improvements and lowering operational costs overall.

4. The rise of ecommerce marketplaces.

Ecommerce marketplaces have been on the rise around the world since the mid-1990s with the launch of giants we know today as Amazon, Alibaba, and others.

By offering a broad selection and extreme convenience to customers, they've been able to quickly scale up through innovation and optimization on the go. Amazon in particular is known for its unique growth strategy that has helped them achieve mass-adoption and record-breaking sales. But Amazon doesn't do this alone. As of 2017, 51% of products sold on Amazon were sold by third-party sellers (i.e. not Amazon). Those sellers also make high profits from the sales on the marketplace, though they are required to follow strict rules enforced by Amazon.

5. Supply chain management has evolved.

Survey data shows that one of ecommerce's main impacts on supply chain management is that it shortens product life cycles. As a result, producers are presenting deeper and broader assortments as a buffer against price erosion. But, this also means that warehouses are seeing larger amounts of stock in and out of their facilities. In response, some warehousers are now offering value-added services to help make ecommerce and retail operations more seamless and effective.

These services include:

- Separation of stock/storage for online vs. retail sales.
- Different packaging services.
- Inventory/logistics oversight.

6. New jobs are created but traditional retail jobs are reduced.

Jobs related to ecommerce are up 2x over the last five years, far outpacing other types of retail in regard to growth. However, growth in ecommerce jobs is only a small piece of the employment puzzle overall.

A few quick facts on how ecommerce has impacted employment:

• Ecommerce jobs are up 334%, adding 178,000 jobs since 2002

• Most ecommerce jobs are located in medium to large metropolitan areas

• Most ecommerce companies have four or fewer employees

Scholars indicate that ecommerce will continue to directly and indirectly create new jobs in the high-skill domains like the information and software sectors, as well as around increased demand for productivity.

(Total words:1094, taken from: https://www.bigcommerce.com/blog/ecommerce/)

New Words and Expressions

encryption /ɪnˈkrɪpʃən/ n. the activity of converting data or information into code 编码,加密

logistics /ləˈdʒɪstɪks/ n. the practical organization that is needed to make a complicated plan successful when a lot of people and equipment is involved 后勤;物流;组织工作

fulfillment /fʊlˈfɪlmənt/ n. a feeling of satisfaction at having achieved your desires 满足感;成就感;履行;实现

variation /ˌveəriˈeɪʃn/ n. a change, especially in the amount or level of sth. (数量、水平等的)变化,变更,变异

transaction /trænˈzækʃn/ n. a piece of business that is done between people, especially an act of buying or selling(一笔)交易,业务,买卖

available /əˈveɪləbl/ adj. (of things) that you can get, buy or find (东西)可获得的,可购得的,可找到的

categorize /ˈkætəgəraɪz/ v. to put people or things into groups according to what type they are 将……分类,把……加以归类

individual /ˌɪndɪˈvɪdʒuəl/ n. a person considered separately rather than as part of a group 个人 adj. considered separately rather than as part of a group 单独的,个别的

administration /ədˌmɪnɪˈstreɪʃn/ n. the activities that are done in order to plan, organize and run a business, school or other institution(企业、学校等的)管理,行政

retailer /ˈriːteɪlə/ n. a person or business that sells goods to the public 零售商,零售店

wholesaler /ˈhəʊlseɪlə/ n. someone who buys large quantities of goods and resells to merchants rather than to the ultimate customers 批发商

efficiency /ɪˈfɪʃnsi/ n. the quality of doing sth. well with no waste of time or money 效率;效能;功效

mid-tier /mɪdtɪə/ n. a middle row or layer of sth. that has several rows or layers placed one above the other 中档,中档组

maintain /meɪnˈteɪn/ v. to make sth. continue at the same level, standard, etc. 维持，保持

Proper Nouns

  Business-to-Consumer（B2C）　企业对消费者

  Business-to-Business（B2B）　企业对企业

  Consumer-to-Consumer（C2C）　消费者对消费者

  Consumer-to-Business（C2B）　消费者对企业

  Business-to-Administration（B2A）　企业对政府

  Consumer-to-Administration（C2A）　消费者对政府

Reading Task

Task 1 What does the author infer by stating the italicized phrases in the following sentences?

1. Keep in mind that ecommerce has a few different spelling variations. All of these are synonymous and correct—*their use is largely preference-based*.

2. The impact of ecommerce is far and wide *with a ripple effect on* everything from small business to global enterprise and beyond.

3. By offering a broad selection and extreme convenience to customers, they've been able to quickly *scale up* through innovation and optimization on the go.

4. As a result, producers are presenting deeper and broader assortments as *a buffer against price erosion*.

Task 2 Complete the following table about the main points of the text.

What Is Ecommerce
Ecommerce is the buying and selling of goods (or services) _____.
Types of Ecommerce

1. _____.	4. Consumer-to-Business (C2B).
2. _____.	5. Business-to-Administration (B2A).
3. Consumer-to-Consumer (C2C).	6. Consumer-to-Administration (C2A).

The Impact of Ecommerce
1. Large retailers are forced to sell online.
2. Ecommerce helps small businesses sell directly _____.
3. B2B companies start offering B2C-like _____.
4. The rise of ecommerce marketplaces.

Task 3 Decide whether the following statements are true (T) or false (F).

1. B2C ecommerce ecompasses transcations made between a business and business. (   )

2. Customer-to-customer relates to the sale of products or services between customers. (   )

3. Ecommerce has an effect on everything from small business to global enterprise and beyond. (   )

4. Research also didn't indicate that one type of retailer in particular has seen a major impact from the rise of ecommerce: department stores. (   )

5. In 2017, 51% of products sold on Amazon were sold by third-party sellers (i.e. not Amazon). (   )

Task 4 Work in pairs and answer the following questions.

1. What does *ecommerce* refer to, according to the passage?

2. What is the difference between B2C and B2B?

3. What is your inference of the C2C model?

4. Why are large retailers forced to sell online?

5. How does ecommerce help small business sell directly to customers?

6. Can ecommerce help to be against price erosion?

7. How does ecommerce have an effect on jobs?

Task 5 Group Discussion

Nowadays, almost all people like to shop online. What influence does it have on your life? Please talk about it with your partners.

Language Building-up

Task 1 The following expressions are taken from Text A. Translate the following terms from English into Chinese.

electronic commerce

a business-to-consumer transaction

a manufacturer and a wholesaler

global enterprise

user-friendly platforms

medium to large metropolitan areas

Task 2 Translate the following sentences from the passage into Chinese.

1. Most often, business-to-business sales focus on raw materials or products that are repackaged or combined before being sold to

customers.

___

___

2. This would include customer to customer selling relationships like those seen on eBay or Amazon.

___

___

3. Slowly, small business owners are launching ecommerce stores and diversifying their offerings, reaching more customers, and better accommodating customers who prefer online/mobile shopping.

___

___

4. Amazon in particular is known for its unique/growth strategy that has helped them achieve mass-adoption and record-breaking sales.

___

___

Task 3 Complete the following sentences with the correct form of the words in the box.

| fulfillment variation categorize individual |
| available administration efficiency maintain |

1. You can _____ existing software components by language, purpose, type, and function.

2. A child's awareness of being an _____ grows in stages during

the pre-school years.

3. Research shows that relationships, especially friendship and marriage, are key factors of happiness and _____.

4. With such excellent studies _____ for consultation, it should be easy to avoid the pitfalls.

5. The institutions have realized they need to change their culture to improve _____ and service.

6. The survey found a wide _____ in the prices charged for canteen food.

7. He has _____ that the money was donated for international purpose.

8. The _____ is in the process of drawing up a peace plan.

Task 4 Translate the following paragraph into English.

电子商务是以信息网络技术为手段,以商品交换为中心的商务活动;也可理解为在互联网、企业内部网和增值网上以电子交易方式进行交易活动和相关服务的活动。它是传统商业活动各环节的电子化、网络化和信息化。电子商务可提供网上交易和管理等全过程的服务,因此它具有广告宣传、咨询洽谈、网上订购、网上支付、电子账户、服务传递、意见征询和交易管理等各项功能。

Passage B   Hot Trends That Will Continue to Change Your Ecommerce Horizons in 2018

Recent data released by the U. S. Census Bureau shows impressive growth for the ecommerce industry, with online revenue steadily eating into an additional 1.5 percent of total retail sales every year over the past several years.

As retail giants and traditional storefronts continue to cut costs or even shut their doors, we can't help but wonder how the future of ecommerce will look. Between the announcements that Toys R Us was filing for bankruptcy and Walmart had halted hiring for the holiday season, it's clear that digital commerce is putting a big dent in its brick-and-mortar competitors.

So what are the next growth frontiers in online retail? The developments that helped make 2017 such a landmark year in the trajectory of the industry may be one indicator along, with several predictions I've posed below on where things are headed over the year ahead.

1. A Larger International Market

While many merchants may be worried only about reaching buyers in their own backyards, consider the inevitable growth of the international ecommerce market. Shoppers have no problem going beyond borders—buying from U.S. vendors, for example—as long as those vendors' sites and storefronts can translate their copy, allow multiple types of payment and utilize shipping solutions that aren't outrageously priced.

In fact, a recent Nielsen reported that 57 percent of shoppers polled had purchased from an overseas retailer within the past six months.

Selling to an international market may seem like a huge

undertaking, and can indeed be overwhelming if you don't have the right platform or tools available. But, thanks to solutions like BigCommerce, sellers can handle global markets in more than 150 countries. The integrations offered make it easy to accept payments through a number of gateways, including PayPal and Stripe, without transaction fees.

Shipping calculators and integrations also make it easy to ship products internationally and to account for the necessary shipping fees and taxes, without biting into your profit margin. Your store will display in nearly any language with nearly any currency, so no matter where your customers are, your store will provide a positive customer experience.

2. Expect the "Little Guy" to Look Beyond Amazon

Amazon is projected to make up half of all ecommerce sales in the United States by 2021, a sobering statistic for smaller merchants. That said, third-party merchants accounted for an impressive $11.98 billion in sales on Amazon during the first quarter of 2017 alone, signaling the power smaller brands have to take advantage of the ecommerce behemoth's platform.

With Walmart heavily promoting its own marketplace platform for third-party sellers, expect more retail giants to hop on board, to appeal to smaller merchants in the coming months and years.

Using a system like ChannelApe allows you to connect all of your ecommerce integrations into your current systems. This way, you can list your products for sale in a number of third-party markets like those on Amazon and Walmart, without potentially overselling a product.

Of course, it can be difficult and time-consuming to track inventory and manage orders from one platform to the next, so these integrations can automate and simplify the process. If you sell a product on Amazon or Walmart, your inventory will update so the same product isn't sold from another marketplace or customer touchpoint. This streamlines your entire operation, giving you more time to focus on other areas of your business.

3. The Power of Personalization

Marketing personalization is a two-way street. Merchants have the ability to gather more data on their customers and prospects than ever before. Meanwhile, personalization has become an expectation of the modern consumer.

Personalized shopping experiences based on demographics, previous buying behavior and browsing history are also just the start.

Personalization is easy when you have access to the right data. Figuring it out all on your own takes time. That's where a platform like Evergage becomes essential to ecommerce success. It's a real-time personalization platform that combines behavioral analytics with your customer data and advanced machine learning.

This allows you to interact with each person who visits your store so you can deliver a truly personalized and individualized experience. You'll automatically deliver personalized content and product recommendations and can use split-testing to optimize your conversion rates. You'll be able to reduce shopping-cart abandonment and improve customer loyalty.

4. More Chatbot-Powered Conversations

According to data from eMarketer, more than half of today's social media users prefer to use messenger Apps to connect with brands, rather than turn to email, phone, or a traditional live chat. Enter the chatbot, which is able to reach customers and respond to requests in real-time, learn more about them and personalize their shopping experience based on their responses.

Moreover, chatbots can engage with shoppers, without requiring them to install a native App. Chatbots integrate with platforms such as Skype, Kik and Facebook Messenger.

Though chatbots are doing a great job, so much so that research shows that 35 percent of consumers want more chatbots, they do lack one key element. And that element is the ability to empathize. That's why it's important to have a human customer service representative standing by.

Even so, millennials say they are ready to spend $618 via a chatbot. That's an amazing income stream for ecommerce store owners.

If the idea of building a chatbot for your ecommerce operation seems daunting, you can turn to a platform like Pandorabots. It helps you build smart chatbots for ecommerce. You can use the basic platform to build and learn as you go, and when you're ready to execute, you can move it over to artificial intelligence as a service (AIaaS), which allows you to integrate the chatbot into your applications. You can build a virtual agent to your specifications, and add an avatar or speech capabilities. Best of all, it's free.

5. Increased Protection Against Fraud

Retailers lose billions of dollars annually to fraud, signaling the need for merchants to protect themselves and their customers alike. With security already on the minds of consumers at large, expect a heavier emphasis on security from specialized services and storefront platforms. While there are already ways for merchants to prevent fraud, expect security to become a bigger priority in the coming years.

CyberSource's 2017 *Online Fraud Benchmark* report showed that 58 percent of merchants polled considered their address verification service to be one of their three most effective fraud-prevention tools. Other services considered useful were for card verification numbers and device fingerprinting. Only 25 percent of merchants considered negative lists and two-factor phone authentication among the most effective tools.

Some 62 percent of merchants called the chargeback rate the most important key performance indicator. Manual review was also seen as helpful to avoid fraud, but it can be costly. Seventy-nine percent of businesses used manual review, and on average, they reviewed 25 percent of their orders. The manual reviews account for the majority of the fraud management budget.

Fortunately for businesses, there's a solution that assists with fraud prevention and damage control. Chargeback allows you to bring all of your data sources together, which allows you to spot fraud before it occurs… and when you can't, you can take control after the fraudulent transaction happens. That way, you can refund the customer, prevent order fulfillment and reroute shipments.

On the Horizon

In the coming years, we'll see more merchants expanding outside of their native countries to provide their products and services to a more global market. It will be easier to build brand awareness and bring in new customers through a variety of third-party marketplaces while providing a personalized shopping experience. Merchants who want to stay on the cutting edge will need to integrate chatbots and take steps to curb and prevent fraud.

(Total words: 1300, taken from: https://www.entrepreneur.com/article/316140)

New Words and Expressions

release /rɪˈliːs/ v. to let sb./sth. come out of a place where they have been kept or trapped 释放,放出,放走

revenue /ˈrevənjuː/ n. the money that a government receives from taxes or that an organization, etc. receives from its business 财政收入,税收收入,收益

storefront /ˈstɔːfrʌnt/ n. a room at the front of a shop/store 店面,铺面,铺面房

bankruptcy /ˈbæŋkrʌptsi/ n. a state of complete lack of some abstract property 破产,倒闭

dent /dent/ n. a hollow place in a hard surface, usually caused by sth. hitting it 凹痕,凹坑,凹部

landmark /ˈlændmɑːk/ n. something, such as a large building, that you can see clearly from a distance and that will help you to know where you are 陆标,地标

inevitable /ɪnˈevɪtəbl/ adj. that you cannot avoid or prevent 不可避免的,不能防止的

poll /pəʊl/ v. (usually passive) to ask a large number of members of the public what they think about sth. 对……进行民意调查

undertaking /ˌʌndəˈteɪkɪŋ/ n. a task or project, especially one that is important and/or difficult (重大或艰巨的)任务,项目,事业,企业

overwhelming /ˌəʊvəˈwelmɪŋ/ adj. very great or very strong; so powerful that you cannot resist it or decide how to react 巨大的;压倒性的;无法抗拒的

platform /ˈplætfɔːm/ n. a raised level surface, for example one that equipment stands on or is operated from 平台

account for If something accounts for a particular fact or situation, it causes or explains it. 导致;解释

simplify /ˈsɪmplɪfaɪ/ v. to make sth. easier to do or understand 使简化,使简易

streamline /ˈstriːmlaɪn/ v. to give sth. a smooth shape so that it can move quickly and easily through air or water 使成流线型

demographics /ˌdeməˈɡræfɪks/ n. data relating to the population and different groups within it 人口统计数据

fraudulent /ˈfrɔːdjələnt/ adj. intended to cheat sb., usually in order to make money illegally 欺骗的，欺诈的

Proper Nouns

 Toys R Us　玩具反斗城

 Walmart　沃尔玛百货有限公司

 third-party market　第三方市场

 PayPal　贝宝公司

 AIaaS (artificial intelligence as a service)　人工智能即服务

Reading Task

Task 1 What does the author infer by stating the italicized phrases in the following sentences?

1. Between the announcements that Toys R Us was filing for bankruptcy and Walmart had halted hiring for the holiday season, it's clear that digital commerce is putting *a big dent* in its brick-and-mortar competitors.

2. The integrations offered make it easy to accept payments through *a number of gateways*, including PayPal and Stripe, without transaction fees.

3. Amazon is projected to make up half of all ecommerce sales in the United States by 2021, *a sobering statistic* for smaller merchants.

4. Marketing personalization is *a two-way street*. Merchants have the ability to gather more data on their customers and prospects than

ever before. Meanwhile, personalization has become an expectation of the modern consumer.

Task 2 Work in pairs and answer the following questions.

1. What advantages does it bring thanks to solutions like BigCommerce?

2. How do retail giants hop on board and appeal to smaller merchants?

3. What ability do merchants have to gather more than ever before?

4. What do more than half of today's social media users prefer to use to connect with brands?

Language Building-up

Task 1 Translate the following sentences from the passage into Chinese.

1. As retail giants and traditional storefronts continue to cut costs or even shut their doors, we can't help but wonder how the future of ecommerce will look.

_____

_____

2. Your store will display in nearly any language with nearly any currency, so no matter where your customers are, your store will provide a positive customer experience.

_____

_____

3. If the idea of building a chatbot for your ecommerce operation seems daunting, you can turn to a platform like Pandorabots.

4. While there are already ways for merchants to prevent fraud, expect security to become a bigger priority in the coming years.

Task 2 Paraphrase the following sentences from the passage.

1. Selling to an international market may seem like a huge undertaking, and can indeed be overwhelming if you don't have the right platform or tools available.

2. Retailers lose billions of dollars annually to fraud, signaling the need for merchants to protect themselves and their customers alike.

3. Fortunately for businesses, there's a solution that assists with fraud prevention and damage control.

4. In the coming years, we'll see more merchants expanding outside of their native countries to provide their products and services to a more global market.

Part Three Academic Writing

Theme-related Writing

On the basis of what you have learned from this unit, write an essay entitled "Ecommerce brings influence to my life". You should write at least 150 words but no more than 200 words.

Unit 5　Human-Computer Interaction

Part One Academic Reading Skills

Identifying the Supporting Details

As we have noted, the main idea is usually strengthened by such details as examples, reasons, facts, and other specific details. All of these specific details are called supporting details. Without them, it would be difficult to fully understand the more general main idea.

While the major details explain and develop the main idea, in turn, they are expanded upon by the minor supporting details. An important reading skill is the ability to find these major and minor details, which are needed for the reader to really understand the main idea.

Tips for you to identify the supporting details:

1. Focus on the connectives that delivering examples, reasons and facts, such as *for instance*, *namely*, *including*, *therefore*, *actually*, and so on.

2. Adopt a thinking map or outline helping you to identify and sort

certain points.

3. Pay attention to the location of subtitles, numbers, places, negatives, proper nouns and so on.

Part Two Passage Reading

Passage A Human-Machine Interaction

Pre-reading Task

Directions: *Read the title and discuss the following questions in groups.*

1. What is human-machine interaction (HMI)?

2. Thanks to development of human-machine interaction, application domains benefit a lot. Can you list some of the application domains?

Human-machine interaction with industrial plants and other dynamic technical systems has nowadays been recognized as essential for process safety, quality, and efficiency. It comprises all aspects of interaction and communication between human users and their machines via human-machine interfaces.

The whole system of human users, the human-machine interface, and the machine is the so-called human-machine system (HMS); see Figure 1. Different human user classes may be involved, namely, operators, engineers, maintenance personnel, and managers. They have different but overlapping information needs.

The term "machine" indicates any kind of dynamic technical system (or real-time application), including its automation and decision support equipment and software—and it relates to many diverse application domains.

The automation components of the technical system are denoted as supervision and control systems. They interact directly with the pure technical (production) process. Examples of such processes are a power generation process, a chemical or a discrete-parts production process, an aircraft, a tele-manipulator or a real-time software application.

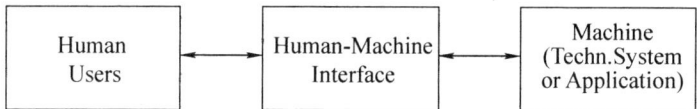

Figure 1: The whole human-machine system (HMS) with human users, human-machine interface, and the machine.

The decision support systems are more advanced, knowledge-based functionalities of the machine which provide advice for the human users.

The application domains include all kinds of industrial, transportation, medical, service, home, and entertainment systems. The more traditional application domains of industrial and transportation systems have nowadays been supplemented by application domains from medical to entertainment systems. All application domains profit from advancements in the development of the human-computer interaction field. Human computer interaction (HCI) is characterized as human interaction with those computer application domains which are not determined by a dynamic process or by real-time constraints, as it is always the case in human-machine interaction (HMI).

The degree of automation in control of dynamic technical systems has substantially been increased over the last decades. This is true for all technical systems such as power plants, industrial production plants, and vehicles and transportation systems. High levels of safety, performance, and efficiency have been achieved by means of the increased use of automatic control. Interestingly enough—however, with no surprise to human factors specialists—the need for improved human-machine communication increased (rather than decreased) with the increased degree of automation. Generally, increased automation does not replace the human users who are interacting with the machine, but shifts the location of the interface between both. The machine as an automated system becomes more complex than one with less automation, leading to more sophisticated structures of supervisory control. Higher complexity and more sophisticated control structures require a new quality of communication and co-operation between human and machine. The role of the human user shifts from that of a controller to that of a supervisor. The human supervisor interacts with the process through one or several layers of computers on which the human-machine interface, the automation, and the decision support functionalities are implemented.

Thus, the functionalities of well-designed human-machine interaction have a long time. Today, it is also more and more followed in industry. Under the perspective of human-centered automation and human-centered design, human-machine interaction appears to be a symbiotic process between the human users and their machines via human-machine interfaces whereby both—machines and interfaces—have properly been designed. The functionalities of both, the machine and the interface, have to be specified and designed with a strong view on human-centeredness, i.e., with respect to user orientation—concerning human cognitive processes, human needs, and human capabilities—and based on goal orientation and task orientation. Then, these functionalities can be implemented as extended automation modules and knowledge-based decision support systems within the machine and as interaction and communication modules within the human-machine interfaces. Computer graphics, multimedia and multimodal displays, as well as knowledge-based and other software technologies offer a wide range of alternative designs for human-machine interfaces, extended automation, and knowledge-based support.

Human-machine interaction is goal-oriented. The overall goals of human-machine systems are mainly (1) productivity goals, (2) safety goals, (3) humanization goals, and (4) environmental compatibility goals. The productivity goals include economic as well as product and production quality goals. The importance of the safety goals is strongly influenced by the application domain. This goal class dominates all others in many large-scale systems and, particularly, in risky systems. The humanization goals comprise team and work organization, job satisfaction, ergonomic compatibility, and cognitive compatibility. The latter includes the sub-goals of transparency and human understanding. The environmental compatibility goals refer to the consumption of energy and material resources as well as to impacts on soil, water, and air.

Human-machine interaction and human-machine systems research require multidisciplinary or interdisciplinary views and approaches. The following three domains contribute to human-machine interaction and systems research: (1) cognitive science and ergonomics (as the human sciences), (2) automation and systems engineering (as the systems sciences), and (3) information and communication engineering (as the computer sciences). Further, organizational and cultural aspects are strongly involved.

Human-machine systems research has now been performed for about 60 years. Nevertheless, it took quite some time before the human-machine systems field became an established and more widely accepted discipline, particularly also in industries. For long time, mainly the aeronautics and astronautics industries and, to a lesser extent, the car manufacturing industries showed some more interest. This situation has now totally changed. It has been recognized that a good symbiosis between human and machine is generally required. Good human-machine interaction and systems designs have gained a high market value for almost all products and services. Consequently, strong needs in industry and society exist today as an important application pull. This influences the human-machine systems field which became mature but continues, at the same time, as an innovative and always further developing research area.

(Total words: 1033, taken from: https://www.eolss.net/Sample-

Chapters/C18/E6-43-37-06.pdf)

New Words and Expressions

comprise /kəmˈpraɪz/ v. to form part of a larger group of people or things 构成,组成

overlap /əʊvəˈlæp/ v. If one thing overlaps another, or if you overlap them, a part of the first thing occupies the same area as a part of the other thing. You can also say that two things overlap. 重叠

denote /dɪˈnəʊt/ v. to represent or be a sign of something 表示(是……的符号、标志等),代表

substantially /səbˈstænʃəli/ adv. used to say that in many ways something is true, the same, different etc. 主要地;大体上,基本上

sophisticated /səˈfɪstɪkeɪtɪd/ adj. A sophisticated machine, system, method etc. is very well designed and very advanced, and often works in a complicated way. (机器、系统、方法等)复杂的,精密的,尖端的

symbiotic /sɪmbaɪˈɒtɪk/ adj. A symbiotic relationship is one in which the people, organizations, or living things involved depend on each other. (人、组织或生物)互相依赖的,共生的

cognitive /ˈkɒɡnɪtɪv/ adj. related to the process of knowing, understanding, and learning something 认知的,认知过程的

ergonomic /ɜːɡəʊˈnɒmɪk/ adj. of or relating to ergonomics 人类工程学的

compatibility /kəmˌpætɪˈbɪlɪtɪ/ n. the ability of one piece of computer equipment to be used with another one, especially when they are made by different companies (计算机设备的)兼容性

symbiosis /ˌsɪmbɪˈəʊsɪs/ n. the relationship between different living things that depend on each other (生物的)共生(关系)

Proper Nouns

HMI   human-machine interaction   人机界面，又称用户界面或使用者界面

HCI   human computer interaction   人机交互

Reading Task

Task 1 Fill in the following chart with relevant information to understand major and minor supporting details of the text.

Subject	Major supporting details	Minor supporting details
Human-Machine interaction	It relates to diverse application domains.	1. The application domains include all kinds of industrial, _____, medical, _____, home, and entertainment systems. 2. Traditional application domains have been _____ by application domains from _____ to _____ systems.
	The functionalities of well-designed human-machine interaction have a long time.	1. The _____ of automation in control of dynamic technical systems has substantially been increased. 2. The _____ for improved human-machine communication increased. 3. _____ have to be specified and designed with a strong view on _____.
	Overall goals and views/approaches of human-machine system.	1. Goals of _____, safety, _____, environmental compatibility. 2. Views/approaches: _____ and ergonomics, automation and _____, information and _____.

106

Task 2 Complete the following table.

Human-machine interaction	Human users like _____ have different but overlapping information needs. The machine relates to many _____ application domains.
	The human-machine interface, the automation, and the decision support functionalies are implemented on the human supervisor interacts through _____.
	Human-machine interaction seems to be a _____ process between the human users and their machines via human-machine interfaces.
	The goals of human-machine systems are mainly _____ goals, _____ goals, _____ goals, and _____ goals.
	Human-machine interaction and human-machine systems research require _____ or _____ views and approaches.
	HCI has been recognized as a good _____ between human and machine.

Task 3 Decide whether the following statements are true (T) or false (F).

1. Human users and machine interact directly with the pure technical (production) process. (   )

2. In the case of human-machine interaction (HMI) human interact with those computer application domains which are not determined by a dynamic process or by real-time constraints. (   )

3. The degree of all technical systems has substantially been increased over the last decades. (   )

4. The more complex the automated-system machine is, the more sophisticated the structures of supervisory control becomes. (   )

5. Strong needs in industry and society today pull the human-machine system field to be a mature and developing research area. (   )

6. Human-machine systems field has not been an established and more widely accepted discipline especially in industries. (   )

Task 4 Work in pairs and answer the following questions.

1. "They interact directly with the pure technical (production) process." (Para. 4) What does "*they*" refer to?

2. "Interestingly enough—however, with no surprise to human factors specialists—the need for improved human-machine communication increased (rather than decreased) with the increased degree of automation." (Para. 7) Why does the author use dashes here?

3. Human users change their roles to a supervisor instead of a controller. What does a supervisor do?

4. In what aspects does the author illustrate his point that "*the functionalities of well-designed human-machine interaction have a long time.*"?

5. "Today, it is also more and more followed in industry." (Para. 8) How do you understand "*followed*" here?

Task 5 Group Discussion

Human-machine interaction has nowadays been recognized as essential for process safety, quality, and efficiency. What's more, good human-machine interaction and system design have gained a high market value for almost all products and services. Work in groups of 3－4 and come up with illustrations as many as possible.

Language Building-up

Task 1 The following expressions are taken from Text A. Translate the following terms from English into Chinese.

human-machine system (HMS)

human-machine interaction (HMI)

human computer interaction (HCI)

real-time

tele-manipulator

functionality

interdisciplinary

ergonomics

Task 2 Complete the following sentences with the correct form of the words and expressions in the box.

| namely   with respect to   leading to   profit from |
| nevertheless   consequently   rather than   by means of |

1. However, parents, teachers and students take on quite different views and, _____, they seem not to have reached any compromises yet.

2. There is something of a chicken and egg problem _____ a reference architecture.

109

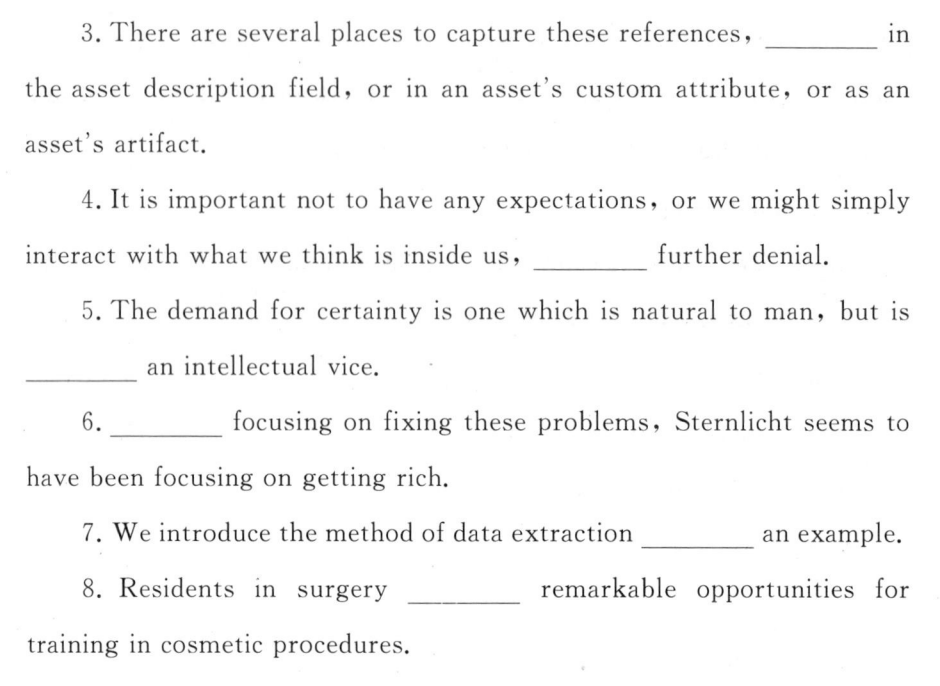

3. There are several places to capture these references, _____ in the asset description field, or in an asset's custom attribute, or as an asset's artifact.

4. It is important not to have any expectations, or we might simply interact with what we think is inside us, _____ further denial.

5. The demand for certainty is one which is natural to man, but is _____ an intellectual vice.

6. _____ focusing on fixing these problems, Sternlicht seems to have been focusing on getting rich.

7. We introduce the method of data extraction _____ an example.

8. Residents in surgery _____ remarkable opportunities for training in cosmetic procedures.

Task 3 Translate the following paragraph into English.

德国研究人员正在开发一种全新的可移动交互系统,此系统能够通过视觉存贮设备将视觉信号转换为命令,有望能全面代替键盘和显示器。这种设备是一个小型的、能够放在胸前的电脑,其摄像头能捕捉到手部运动,从而转换成对应的命令执行。例如人们可以用手在空中画出各种图形,或选择空中不同的点来构型,此交互系统可以立即将这些手上动作转化成图形或操作命令,就像《钢铁侠2》里的托尼·斯达克在自己实验室里用手在空中挥动便能操作电脑一般。在不久的将来,你在空中画几个数字就能表示在拨打电话,或者在空中点几下就表示在打键盘,一切就将变得美妙无比。

Passage B Human-Machine Interaction Now and in the Future

Technologies and computer systems are assuming important tasks in everyday life and industry—visibly or behind the scenes. Sensors and interfaces allow them to be operated. But how do users and computers communicate with and respond to each other? Machines can be controlled by touch, voice, gestures or virtual reality (VR) glasses.

We have long got used to interaction between human and machine: A smartphone user asks the digital assistant what the weather's going to be like and it replies. At home, the human voice controls smart thermostats or commands the intelligent speaker to play "Summer of '69". A few gestures on the smartphone's touch screen are enough to view photos from Kenya and enlarge individual pictures. Chatbots conduct automatic dialogs with customers in messengers. Engineers in industry use VR glasses to enable them to walk through planned factory buildings. For all that to be possible, you need human-machine interaction (HMI) that works.

What Is Human-Machine Interaction?

HMI is all about how people and automated systems interact and communicate with each other. That has long ceased to be confined to just traditional machines in industry and now also relates to computers, digital systems or devices for the Internet of Things (IoT). More and more devices are connected and automatically carry out tasks. Operating all of these machines, systems and devices needs to be intuitive and must not place excessive demands on users.

How Does Human-Machine Interaction Work?

Smooth communication between people and machines requires interfaces: the place where or action by which a user engages with the machine. Simple examples are light switches or the pedals and steering wheel in a car: An action is triggered when you flick a switch, turn the steering wheel or step on a pedal. However, a system can also be controlled by text being keyed in, a mouse, touch screens, voice or gestures.

The devices are either controlled directly: Users touch the smart phone's screen or issue a verbal command. Or the systems automatically identify what people want: Traffic lights change color on their own when a vehicle drives over the inductive loop in the road's surface. Other technologies are not so much there to control devices, but rather to complement our sensory organs. One example of that is virtual reality glasses. There are also digital assistants: Chatbots, for instance, reply automatically to requests from customers and keep on learning.

Chatbots and Digital Assistants: Artificial Intelligence and Chatbots in Human-Machine Interaction

Eliza, the first chatbot, was invented in the 1960s, but soon ran up against its limitations: It couldn't answer follow-up questions. That's different now. Today's chatbots "work" in customer service and give written or spoken information on departure times or services, for example. To do that, they respond to keywords, examine the user's input and reply on the basis of preprogramed rules and routines. Modern chatbots work with artificial intelligence. Digital assistants like Google Home and Google Assistant are also chatbots.

They all learn from the requests and thus expand their repertoire on their own, without direct intervention by a human. They can remember earlier conversations, make connections and expand their vocabulary. Google's voice assistant can deduce queries from their context with the aid of artificial intelligence, for example. The more chatbots understand and the better they respond, the closer we come to communication that resembles a conversation between two people. Big data also plays a role here: If more information is available to the bots, they can respond in a more specific way and give more appropriate replies.

Chatbots and digital assistants will grow in importance moving ahead. The market research company IHS predicts a growth rate of 46 percent in the coming years solely for assistants, such as Amazon's smart speaker Echo.

The Path to Refined Voice Control

Users control systems such as Alexa, Google Assistant, Google Home or Microsoft's Cortana with their voice. They no longer have to touch a display—all they need to do is say the codeword that activates the assistant (e. g. "Alexa") and then, for example "Turn the volume down" or "Reduce the temperature in the bedroom." That's less effort for users—and more intuitive. "The human voice is the new interface," prophesied Microsoft's CEO Satya Nadella back in 2014.

Yet voice recognition is still not perfect. The assistants do not understand every request because of disturbance from background noise. In addition, they're often not able to distinguish between a human voice and a TV, for example. The voice recognition error rate in 2013 was 23 percent, according to the U. S. Consumer Technology Association (CTA). In 2016, Microsoft's researchers brought that down to below six percent for the first time. But that's still not enough.

Infineon intends to significantly improve voice control together with the British semiconductor manufacturer XMOS. The company supplies voice processing modules for devices in the Internet of Things. A new solution presented by Infineon and XMOS at the beginning of 2017 uses smart microphones. It enables assistants to pinpoint the human voice in the midst of other noises: A combination of XENSIV™ radar and silicon microphone sensors from Infineon identifies the position and the distance of the speaker from the microphones, with far field voice processing technology from XMOS being used to capture speech.

The Path to Gesture Control

Gesture control has a number of advantages over touch screens: Users don't have to touch the device, for example, and can thus issue commands from a distance. Gesture control is an alternative to voice control, not least in the public sphere. After all, speaking with your smart wearable on the subway might be unpleasant for some and provoke unwanted attention. Gesture control also opens up the third dimension, away from two-dimensional user interfaces.

Google and Infineon have developed a new type of gesture control by the name of "Soli". They use radar technology for this: Infineon's radar chip can receive waves reflected from the user's finger. That means if someone moves their hand, it's registered by the chip. Google algorithms then process these signals. That even works in the dark, remotely or with dirty fingers. The same uniform hand movements apply to all Soli devices. The Soli chip can be used in all possible devices, such as loudspeakers or smart watches. "Mature algorithms that trace patterns of movement and touch, as well as tiny, highly integrated radar chips, can enable a large range of applications," says Andreas Urschitz. This technology could dispense with the need for all buttons and switches in the future.

(Total Words:1143, taken from: www.infineon.com)

New Words and Expressions

sensor /ˈsensə/ n. a piece of equipment used for discovering the presence of light, heat, movement etc. (探测光、热、活动等的)传感器,感应装置

thermostat /ˈθɜːməstæt/ n. an instrument used for keeping a room or a machine at a particular temperature 恒温器

intuitive /ɪnˈtjuːɪtɪv/ adj. An intuitive idea is based on a feeling rather than on knowledge or facts. (想法)(出于)直觉的

trigger /ˈtrɪɡə/ v. to make something happen very quickly, especially a series of events 引发,激发(尤指一系列事件)

inductive /ɪnˈdʌktɪv/ adj. connected with electrical or magnetic induction 电感的，磁感的

loop /luːp/ n. a shape like a curve or a circle made by a line curving back towards itself, or a piece of wire, string etc. that has this shape 圈，环

repertoire /ˈrepətwɑː/ n. the total number of things that someone or something is able to do 全部技能

deduce /dɪˈdjuːs/ v. to use the knowledge and information you have in order to understand something or form an opinion about it 推论，推断；演绎

prophesy /ˈprɒfɪsaɪ/ v. to say what will happen in the future, especially using religious or magical knowledge 预言

provoke /prəˈvəʊk/ v. to cause a reaction or feeling, especially a sudden one 激起，引起

algorithm /ˈælɡərɪð(ə)m/ n. a set of instructions that are followed in a fixed order and used for solving a mathematical problem, making a computer program etc. 演算法，计算程序

Proper Nouns

  VR virtual reality 虚拟现实

  IoT Internet of Things 物联网

  CTA Consumer Technology Association 消费者技术协会

Reading Task

Task 1 Work in pairs and answer the following questions.

1. "Technologies and computer systems are assuming important tasks in everyday life and industry—visibly or behind the scenes."(Para. 1) What does "*visibly or behind the scenes*" mean?

2. How many kinds of devices and techniques does the author mainly put forward in the passage? And what are they?

3. "An action is triggered when you flick a switch, turn the steering wheel or step on a pedal."(Para. 4) Guess the meaning of "*flick*".

Language Building-up

Task 1 Translate the following sentences from the passage into Chinese.

1. That has long ceased to be confined to just traditional machines in industry and now also relates to computers, digital systems or devices for the Internet of Things (IoT).

2. The more chatbots understand and the better they respond, the closer we come to communication that resembles a conversation between two people.

3. A new solution presented by Infineon and XMOS at the beginning of 2017 uses smart microphones. It enables assistants to pinpoint the

human voice in the midst of other noises.

4. Gesture control is an alternative to voice control, not least in the public sphere. After all, speaking with your smart wearable on the subway might be unpleasant for some and provoke unwanted attention.

5. Mature algorithms that trace patterns of movement and touch, as well as tiny, highly integrated radar chips, can enable a large range of applications.

Task 2 Paraphrase the following sentences from the passage.

1. Technologies and computer systems are assuming important tasks in everyday life and industry—visibly or behind the scenes.

2. Operating all of these machines, systems and devices needs to be intuitive and must not place excessive demands on users.

3. Chatbots and digital assistants will grow in importance moving

ahead.

4. This technology could dispense with the need for all buttons and switches in the future.

Part Three Academic Writing

Theme-related Writing

On the basis of what you have learned from this unit, write an essay entitled "What influence human-computer interaction exerts on your usual life?". You should write at least 150 words but no more than 200 words.

Unit 6　Big Data

Part One Academic Reading Skills

Dealing with Unfamiliar Words

When coming through unfamiliar words in reading, students can guess the meaning according to the context clues such as a sentence or a paragraph. These clues refer to:

1. Synonym clues. A sentence with a difficult word often contains a more familiar word to make it easy to understand. Usually a synonym clue appears to be of the same part of speech as the new word, and is set apart by commas, dashes or parentheses.

2. Antonym clues. Words or phrases like "or","but","while","as opposed to"and "on the other hand"etc. often signal antonym clues.

3. Example clues. It refers to a word or a phrase that illustrates the unfamiliar word rather than defining it. Students can use the examples to find the correct meaning.

Part Two Passage Reading

Passage A　Creating Value in Health Care Through Big Data

Pre-reading Task

Directions: *Read the title and discuss the following questions in groups.*

1. Have you ever heard of big data?

2. Can you describe some of the major changes that big data has brought us?

What Is Big Data?

No single widely accepted definition of big data appears to be available. However, at least three defining features of it—the three Vs—seem to be generally accepted: volume, variety, and velocity.

Volume is a key characteristic of big data. Massive amounts of data strain the capacity and capability of traditional data storage, management, and retrieval systems such as data warehouses. Big data requires flexible and easily expandable data storage and management solutions.

The second characteristic is variety. Health care data today come in many formats, such as the structured and free-text data captured by EHRs, diagnostic images, and data streaming from social media and mobile applications. However, much of this information is not put to use to improve health or health care. For example, less than 15 percent of health data in EHRs might be entered in structured data fields that allow those data to be analyzed using traditional retrieval and analysis methods. Big-data approaches enable the efficient linking and analyses of disparately formatted data to answer particular operational, business, or research questions.

The third characteristic is velocity. Most traditional health IT infrastructures are not able to process and analyze massive amounts of constantly refreshed, differently formatted data in real time. Big-data infrastructure makes it possible to manage data more flexibly and quickly than has been the case, as we explain below.

More identically formatted data are available for analyses than ever before. For example, the Centers for Medicare and Medicaid Services (CMS) is making Medicare claims data available to researchers and what the Affordable Care Act refers to as "qualified entities" for analysis. Analyzing these data together with claims data from private insurers can offer significant benefits. However, we would not characterize these efforts as leveraging big data's potential. Only if CMS data were combined with differently formatted data (for example, information from EHRS) and rapidly analyzed would the three Vs of big data be achieved and big data's full potential realized.

Big Data's Potential Value

Big data may have the potential to create approximately $300 billion annually in value in the health care sector, two-thirds of which would be generated by lowering health care expenditures. Big data has already demonstrated its economic and clinical value on multiple occasions.

First, the delivery of personalized medicine (individualized diagnoses and treatments based on a patient's detailed risk profile) has been demonstrated for care of patients with cancer or other conditions.

Second, the use of clinical decision support systems has been enhanced by the automated analysis of x-rays, computed tomography (CT) scan images, and magnetic resonance imaging (MRI) images and the mining (described below) of medical literature to tailor treatments to individual patients risk profiles.

Third, reliance on patient-generated data has been demonstrated using mobile devices to tailor diagnostic and treatment decisions as well as educational messages to support desired patient behaviors. For example, the Veterans Health Administration has launched a number of mobile health care initiatives that target specific patients and providers through the rapid collection and analysis of patient-generated data.

Fourth, big data-driven population health analyses have revealed patterns that might have been missed had smaller batches of uniformly formatted data been analyzed instead. One example is the Durkheim Project, a collaboration between the Veterans Health Administration and Facebook, which is using real-time prediction software to analyze voluntary, opt-in data from veterans' social media accounts and mobile phones for suicide risk prevention.

Finally, big-data tools for fraud detection and prevention, such as those used by CMS, have replaced earlier manual documentation processes. These tools have generated over $4 billion dollars in recovered costs in 2011 alone.

IT Infrastructure Required for Big Data

Electronic health care data are beginning to be available in massive amounts. For example, 85 percent of US hospitals have already adopted an EHR system, and most physicians' offices have started to digitize patients' records.

However, for health organizations to rely on big data, enabling IT infrastructure has to be available. Installing such infrastructure and its components is becoming increasingly less expensive. Nonetheless, the installation still requires a significant investment of time (including time spent in training) and money, and it involves lost productivity during the transition process.

In addition, to be successful with big data, organizations need to develop processes and policies that accommodate new protocols, time requirements, risk factors, and mandates for managing data, especially in the area of privacy and security.

Most health IT systems rely on large data warehouses that have a static organization and a blueprint (or data schema) for how to construct a database. Sometimes long and complex processes collectively known as "extract, transform, and load" are required to transfer data from sources such as EHR systems into a data warehouse for analysis.

With big-data IT infrastructure, data can be rapidly ingested; tagged to indicate data properties, including origin; and stored indefinitely in a large, open information space called a "data lake." The data lake can accommodate differently formatted data elements, such as patients' names, laboratory values, documents (including progress notes, discharge instructions, and Clinical Document Architecture documents such as summaries of care that are encoded in Extensible Markup Language), and electrocardiograms and MRIs. New data and formats, such as streaming data from implanted pacemakers or Twitter data feeds, can be added without having to be transformed into uniform formats.

To answer a specific question with a particular analytic approach, analysts create a schema that links the appropriate items in the data lake. There can be as many schemas as there are questions, and schemas can be changed without affecting the raw data.

This approach takes advantage of technologies that are not available with data warehousing or the other traditional ways of managing databases that are still predominant in many health organizations. For example, current approaches to measuring the costs of care rely on payment claims records from data warehouses. Augmenting these analyses with clinical data from EHRs might make it possible to use episode grouping approaches that have higher validity and reliability than current approaches have. However, the static model of claims data in a traditional data warehouse is not conducive to this type of analysis, and adding clinical data often means having to unload the data in the warehouse and execute a new extract, transform, and load process.

In contrast, researchers conducting a cost-of-care analysis in a data lake could simply add new clinical records, queries, and algorithms (or mathematical formulas for solving the problems). The online Appendix provides additional information about health IT infrastructure elements needed to accommodate big data.

Keeping Track of Data Provenance

Big data offers many ways for organizations to tag and track the origin and use of data, as well as who is allowed to access the data. The ability to keep track of data's provenance (the history of the data's origin, ownership, use, and modification) can facilitate essential operations, such as meeting a state's legal requirements about how long data must be stored.

In addition, the storage of tagged data in a data lake gives health care organizations the ability to use original data for repeated analyses to verify findings or identify problems. One example involves the analyses required to support new health care payment models. Organizations using these models may need to be able to adjust payments based on combinations of clinical quality and financial (that is, claims) data. If results from one set of data do not match results from another—say, the patients identified by diagnosis relying on laboratory values, such as blood sugar levels, in clinical records do not match those identified by International Classification of Diseases (ICD) codes in the claims records—health care organizations may need access to the original data to resolve the conflict.

Protecting Data Security and Privacy

Security and privacy concerns related to big data and an IT infrastructure that is accessed through remote locations—for example, via a data cloud and services hosted in the cloud—have presented a significant barrier to the adoption of big-data approaches. Some institutions have been experimenting with "private clouds," using Dropbox or other tools to share protected health information. However, private clouds are limited in terms of elasticity and economies of scale.

An alternative that has arisen to address these limitations is the cloud service provider (CSP). Flexibility and elasticity are built into CSPs' business models. When more computing or storage capacity is needed, a CSP client can procure it almost instantaneously, pay for only what is needed, and then remove the extra capacity if it is no longer required.

For a number of reasons, CSPs may also be able to address data privacy and security concerns more effectively and efficiently than individual can. First, CSPs have already made extensive investments in security measures that could benefit additional organizations at no extra cost. Economies of scale and scope enable CSPs to maintain defenses against cyber attacks or data hackers that may be more sophisticated than defenses that a single health care institution can afford.

Second, CSPs typically rely on up-to-date tools that support stringent security enforcement. For instance, the open-source application Accumulo, originally developed to support national intelligence work, uses sophisticated cryptographic methods to place security tags on every piece of data to assign specific access rights to specific users.

Such applications could enable health care organizations to place different levels of security on different types of data, from demographic information to highly sensitive health data related to substance abuse and sexually transmitted diseases. This would provide the organizations with additional control over the ability to share information without compromising patients' privacy or releasing proprietary data.

(Total words: 1589, taken from: *Creating Value In Health Care Through Big Data: Opportunities And Policy Implications* by Joachim Roski, George W. Bo-Linn, and Timothy A. Andrews.)

New Words and Expressions

velocity /vəˈlɒsəti/ n. distance travelled per unit time 速度

retrieval /riˈtriːvəl/ n. (computer science) the operation of accessing information from the computer's memory 检索;恢复;取回;拯救

leverage /'lev(ə)rɪdʒ/ v. investing with borrowed money as a way to amplify potential gains (at the risk of greater losses) 利用;举债经营

medicare /'mɛdɪˌkɛr/ n. health care for the aged; a federally administered system of health insurance available to persons aged 65 and over(美、加)医疗保险

clinical /'klɪnɪk(ə)l/ adj. relating to a clinic or conducted in or as if in a clinic and depending on direct observation of patients 临床的,诊所的

tomography /təˈmɒɡrəfɪ/ n. (medicine) obtaining pictures of the interior of the body X 线断层摄影术

veteran /'vet(ə)r(ə)n/ n. a serviceman who has seen considerable active service 老兵,老手,富有经验的人;老运动员

uniformly /'juːnɪfɔːmlɪ/ adv. in a uniform manner 一致地

static /'stætɪk/ adj. not active or moving 静态的,静电的,静力的

schema /'skiːmə/ n. a schematic or preliminary plan 模式;计划;图解;概要

ingest /ɪn'dʒest/ vt. serve oneself to, or consume regularly 摄取;咽下;吸收;接待

electrocardiogram /ɪˌlektrəʊ'kɑːdɪəʊɡræm/ n. a graphical recording of the cardiac cycle produced by an electrocardiograph (内科)心电图

pacemaker /'peɪsmeɪkə/ n. a specialized bit of heart tissue that controls the heartbeat (基医)起搏器

episode /'epɪsəʊd/ n. a part of a broadcast serial 情节

provenance /ˈprɒv(ə)nəns/ n. where something originated or was nurtured in its early existence 出处，起源

procure /prəˈkjʊə/ vt. get by special effort 获得，取得；导致

stringent /ˈstrɪn(d)ʒ(ə)nt/ adj. demanding strict attention to rules and procedures 严格的，严厉的；紧缩的，短缺的

cryptographic /ˌkrɪptəˈɡræfɪk/ adj. of or relating to cryptanalysis 关于暗号的，用密码写的

proprietary /prəˈpraɪət(ə)rɪ/ adj. protected by trademark or patent or copyright; made or produced or distributed by one having exclusive rights 所有的，专利的

Proper Nouns

EHRs   Electronic Health Records   电子健康记录

CMS   Centers for Medicare and Medicaid Services   医疗保险和医疗补助服务中心

ICD   International Classification of Diseases   国际疾病分类

CSP   cloud service provider   云服务提供商

Reading Task

Task 1 With the help of context clues, match the italicized words in the sentences with their corresponding meanings in the box.

A. pattern	B. origin	C. old soldier	D. speed
E. strict	F. be dealt with	G. acquire	H. beneficial

1. The third characteristic is *velocity*. Most traditional health IT infrastructures are not able to process and analyze massive amounts of constantly refreshed, differently formatted data in real time.

2. For example, the *Veterans* Health Administration has launched a number of mobile health care initiatives that target specific patients and providers through the rapid collection and analysis of patient-generated data.

3. With big-data IT infrastructure, data can be rapidly *ingested*; tagged to indicate data properties, including origin; and stored indefinitely in a large, open information space called a "data lake."

4. To answer a specific question with a particular analytic approach, analysts create a *schema* that links the appropriate items in the data lake.

5. However, the static model of claims data in a traditional data warehouse is not *conducive* to this type of analysis…

6. The ability to keep track of data's *provenance* can facilitate essential operations.

7. When more computing or storage capacity is needed, a CSP client can *procure* it almost instantaneously, pay for only what is needed, and then remove the extra capacity if it is no longer required.

8. Second, CSPs typically rely on up-to-date tools that support *stringent* security enforcement.

Task 2 Complete the following table about the main points of the text.

Big Data	No single widely accepted definition of big data appears to be available. However, at least three defining features of it—the three Vs— seem to be generally accepted: _____, _____, and _____.
	Big data has already demonstrated its economic and clinical value on multiple occasions, such as the delivery of _____ medicine, the use of _____ support systems.
	To be successful with big data, organizations need to develop _____ and policies that accommodate new _____, time _____, _____ factors, and mandates for _____, especially in the area of _____ and _____.
	Augmenting these analyses with clinical data from EHRs might make it possible to use episode grouping approaches that have higher _____ and _____ than current approaches have.
	Big data offers many ways for organizations to ____ and ____ the origin and use of data, as well as who is allowed to _____ the data. The ability to keep track of data's _____ can facilitate essential operations.
	An alternative that has arisen to address these limitations is the _____. _____ and _____ are built into CSPs' business models.
	Economies of scale and scope enable CSPs to maintain defenses against _____ attacks or data _____ that may be more _____ than defenses that a single health care institution can afford.

Task 3 Decide whether the following statements are true (T) or false (F).

1. Big-data approaches enable the efficient linking and analyses of

disparately formatted data to answer particular operational, business, or research questions. (   )

2. Reliance on patient-generated data can not be demonstrated using mobile devices to tailor diagnostic and treatment decisions as well as educational messages to support desired patient behaviors. (   )

3. Installing IT infrastructure and its components is becoming increasingly more expensive. (   )

4. Big-data tools have generated over $6 billion dollars in recovered costs in 2011 alone. (   )

5. The online Appendix provides additional information about health IT infrastructure elements needed to accommodate big data. (   )

6. The storage of tagged data in a data lake gives health care organizations the ability to use original data for repeated analyses to verify findings or identify problems. (   )

7. CSPs may also be able to address data privacy and security concerns more effectively and efficiently than individual can. (   )

Task 4 Work in pairs and answer the following questions.

1. "No single widely accepted definition of big data appears to be available." (Para. 1) Why does the author use negative sentence?

2. "Big-data infrastructure makes it possible to manage data more flexibly and quickly than has been the case, as we explain below." (Para. 4) What does "*below*" refer to?

3. What occasions have big data already demonstrated its economic and clinical value on?

4. Can you find some examples of the author using brackets to illustrate his points? Why does the author use brackets?

Task 5 Group Discussion

According to the text, we know big data has great potential value and it is widely adopted in many areas. Can you find some aspects in life that are using big data? Work in groups of 3—4 and come up with some examples as many as possible.

Language Building-up

Task 1 The following expressions are taken from Text A. Translate the following terms from English into Chinese.

accommodate new protocols

data warehouses

fraud detection and prevention

implanted pacemakers

retrieval systems

sophisticated cryptographic methods

releasing proprietary data

demographic information

Task 2 Complete the following sentences with the correct form of the words in the box.

| protocol warehouses detection pacemakers |
| retrieval cryptographic proprietary Demographic |

1. She was fitted with a _____ after suffering serious heart trouble.

2. He has become a stickler for the finer observances of Washington _____.

3. This question often turns on whether the manufacturer produces a commodity product or a _____ one and the relative size of the parties.

4. Its real purpose is the launching and _____ of small aeroplane in flight.

5. It provides a single and complete view of customers, partners, products, and business through data _____ or federation.

6. As with any _____ keys, these should be changed periodically.

7. _____ change is another reason why the workforce is greying.

8. He describes efforts to gather evidence about the problem and strengthen capacity for _____ and surveillance.

Task 3 Translate the following paragraph into English.

大数据给互联网带来的是空前的信息大爆炸，它不仅改变了互联网的数据应用模式，还将深深影响着人们的生产生活。深处在大数据时代中的人们，已经认识到大数据已经将数据分析的认识从"向后分析"变成"向前分析"，改变了人们的思维模式，但同时大数据也向我们提出了数据采集、分析和使用等难题。在解决了这些难题的同时，也意味着大数据开始向纵深方向发展。

Passage B Big Data and Its Application

What Is Big Data?

In the business landscape of today, data management can be a major determinant of whether you succeed or fail. Most businesses have begun to realize the importance of incorporating strategies that can transform them through the application of big data. In this endeavor, businesses are realizing that big data is not simply a single technology or technique. Rather, big data is a trend that stretches across numerous fields in business and technology.

Big Data is the term used to refer to initiatives and technologies that comprise of data that is too diverse, fast evolving, and vast for ordinary technologies, infrastructure, and skills to address exhaustively. That is, the volume, velocity and variety of the data is far too great. Despite the complexity of this data, advances in technology are allowing businesses to draw value from big data.

For example, your business can be positioned to track consumer web clicks in order to identify consumers' behavioral trends and modify the business's campaigns, advertisements, and pricing to fit the consumers' persona.

An additional example would be where energy service providers assess household consumption levels in order to predict impending outages and promote more efficient energy consumption.

Additionally, health provision bodies may be able to monitor the spread as well as the emergence of illnesses by analyzing social media data. There are numerous applications of big data, the most noteworthy of which will be discussed a little in the article.

In Understanding and Targeting Consumers

This is among the most popular and publicized areas in which big data is being used. In business, big data helps your business to analyze data and better understand the consumers' behaviors and interests. Your business ought to expand beyond its traditional data sets. By incorporating the use of data obtained from social media, browser logs, and sensor data, you will be able to get a clearer picture of what your consumers need. Once you understand this, your business will be better positioned to create predictive models and position itself to meet consumer needs.

Big data can, therefore, apply in analyzing and understanding your audience's interests. For example, some people are even of the opinion that President Obama's second election win was due to his team's superior ability to use big data analytics to understand the audience's interests and appeal to them. In theory, this is plausible, and big data can be used to predict and influence even events as big and important as government elections. How much more so for your business?

Self-Optimization

Big data does not only apply to your business, but can also apply to you as an individual. You can now benefit from data generated by devices such as smart watches. These devices have the capacity, for example, to monitor the amount of calories you intake in a day, your activity level, as well as your sleep patterns. While the real-time information may be exciting to observe, for example, your calorie intake at the end of the day, the real value lies in analyzing your collective data.

With the analysis of data collected from you over a certain period of time, you will be able to make adjustments in your personal life in order to be more productive, to eat healthy, to acquire sufficient amounts of sleep, and so forth.

Improvement of Health Care

This is another area where big data has played and continues to play a major role. For example, computing big data enables health providers to analyze and decode DNA issues in a matter of minutes. Big data will also allow us to discover diseases faster than would be possible without it. On top of this, big data allows healthcare providers to predict the patterns of diseases and, therefore, measures can be set up to prevent further spread of the diseases.

Apple launched a health App known as ResearchKit. Through such an application, researchers can collect data from individual phones to be compiled for various health studies. For example, as a patient your device may prompt you to indicate how you feel about treatment services.

This data along with that gathered from thousands, if not millions, of other participants will reveal information that compels medical practitioners step up the quality of their services. Data gathered from this application and similar ones, can be used to gather information on specific diseases. For example, information on patients of terminal illnesses can be compiled to be used in the furtherance of research.

In addition, big data is already in use in the monitoring of babies who are premature or sick. Through the recording of each heartbeat as well as the breathing pattern of the babies brought to the unit, infections are detectable way before the onset of physical symptoms. This way, treatment is administered early because every hour counts with such fragile babies. This prompt administration of treatment, therefore, increases the babies' chances of survival.

Security and Law Enforcement Improvement

Another sector where big data is heavily applied is in the enhancement and enablement of law enforcement. Governmental institutions, for example, the NSA in the United States use big data to detect and deter potential terrorist activities. In business, on the other hand, big data analytics can be used for the prevention of cyber attacks and unauthorized access. For the police department, big data tools enable the officers to predict and deter criminal activities.

In 2014, the Chicago Police Department in Illinois, United States, sent out officers to pay a visit to persons that had been identified as most likely to commit crimes. This group of people was generated by a computer through the analysis of big data. The officers visited the individuals on their list, not to interrogate or detain them but to offer them information about jobs and training programs.

The officers also educated these individuals on the consequences of certain crimes and their dynamics. As much as the intentions of the police department were sincere, the exercise was quickly shut down when the public opined that the exercise was "profiling". I recognize the importance of security but I have to agree with that opinion.

Conclusion

Although the era of big data has only recently begun, businesses and governments alike are already taking advantage of it. However, big data can be misused, for example, the Chicago Police Departments initiative in following up on people who were identified as potential criminals through big data analysis may have been done with the best of intentions.

Nonetheless, the initiative can still be considered profiling and a tool through which people can be stigmatized for who they are or their past mistakes. However, big data may very well be a double edged sword because through monitoring of social media activity and analyzing people's likes and interests in big data, terrorist attacks can be averted. Yet this is also an invasion of privacy. Despite this downside, the benefits of big data carry much more weight and its applications in business, health, governance, and beyond should be encouraged.

Big data has been slowly developing over the last few centuries and in the course of the past decade, big data has quickly evolved to become what we know it to be today. One vital point to note is that big data is not only about accumulating and storing massive amounts of information but, more importantly, utilizing that information to solve issues in business as well as in our society.

Big data seems to evolve simultaneously with advancement in

technology. Therefore, as we advance in technology, big data will continue to grow as a field and in volume, possibly to levels we cannot even fathom right now.

(Total words: 1272, taken from: https://www.cleverism.com/brief-history-big-data/)

New Words and Expressions

landscape /ˈlændskeɪp/ n. 风景,景色;(比喻义)舞台

determinant /dɪˈtɜːmɪnənt/ n. a thing that decides whether or how sth. happens 决定因素,决定条件

endeavor /ɪnˈdevə/ n. an attempt to do sth., especially sth. new or difficult 努力,尝试

exhaustively /ɪɡˈzɔːstɪvlɪ/ adv. including everything possible; very thorough or complete 详尽地,彻底地,全面地

persona /pəˈsəʊnə/ n. 形象;人物角色

impending /ɪmˈpendɪŋ/ adj. (usually of an unpleasant event) that is going to happen 即将发生的,迫在眉睫的

outage /ˈaʊtɪdʒ/ n. a period of time when the supply of electricity, etc. is not working 停电(等)期间

plausible /ˈplɔːzəbl/ adj. (of an excuse or explanation) reasonable and likely to be true 有道理的,可信的

prompt /prɒmpt/ vt. to cause sth. to happen 促使,导致,激起

practitioner /prækˈtɪʃənə(r)/ n. a person who works in a profession, especially medicine or law (尤指医学或法律界的)从业人员

onset /ˈɒnset/ n. the beginning of sth., especially sth. unpleasant 开端，发生，肇始

fragile /ˈfrædʒaɪl/ adj. not strong and likely to become ill/sick 虚弱的

deter /dɪˈtɜː(r)/ vt. to make sb. decide not to do sth. or continue doing sth., especially by making them understand difficulties and unpleasant results of their actions 阻止，制止，威慑

cyber /ˈsaɪbə/ adj. 计算机（网络）的，信息技术的

interrogate /ɪnˈterəgeɪt/ vt. to ask sb. a lot of questions over a long period of time, especially in an aggressive way 询问，审问，盘问

detain /dɪˈteɪn/ vt. to keep sb. in an official place, such as a police station, a prison or a hospital, and prevent them from leaving 拘留，扣押

opine /əʊˈpaɪn/ vt. to express a particular opinion 表达，发表（意见）

profiling /ˈprəʊfaɪlɪŋ/ n. the act of collecting useful information about sb./sth. so that you can give a description of them or it（有关人或事物的）资料搜集

stigmatize /ˈstɪgmətaɪz/ vt. to treat sb. in a way that makes them feel that they are very bad or unimportant 使感到羞耻，污蔑

avert /əˈvɜːt/ vt. to prevent sth. bad or dangerous from happening 防止，避免

fathom /ˈfæðəm/ vt. to understand or find an explanation for sth. 理解，彻底了解

Reading Task

Task 1 Work in pairs and answer the following questions.

1. How many applications of big data does the author put forward in the passage? And what are they?

2. Considering that big data has been slowly developing over the last few centuries and in the course of the past decade, why does the author say it has quickly evolved to become what we know it to be today?

3. "However, big data may very well be a double edged sword..." (Para. 18). Why does the author consider big data as a double edged sword?

Language Building-up

Task 1 Translate the following sentences from the passage into Chinese.

1. Big Data is the term used to refer to initiatives and technologies that comprise of data that is too diverse, fast evolving, and vast for ordinary technologies, infrastructure, and skills to address exhaustively.

___

___

2. Your business can be positioned to track consumer web clicks in order to identify consumers' behavioral trends and modify the business's campaigns, advertisements, and pricing to fit the consumers' persona.

___

___

3. While the real-time information may be exciting to observe, for

example, your calorie intake at the end of the day, the real value lies in analyzing your collective data.

4. However, big data may very well be a double edged sword because through monitoring of social media activity and analyzing people's likes and interests in big data, terrorist attacks can be averted.

Task 2 Paraphrase the following sentences from the passage.

1. Big data does not only apply to your business, but can also apply to you as an individual.

2. This data along with that gathered from thousands, if not millions, of other participants will reveal information that compels medical practitioners step up the quality of their services.

3. Nonetheless, the initiative can still be considered profiling and a tool through which people can be stigmatized for who they are or their past mistakes.

4. Therefore, as we advance in technology, big data will continue to grow as a field and in volume, possibly to levels we cannot even fathom right now.

Part Three Academic Writing

Theme-related Writing

On the basis of what you have learned from this unit, write an essay entitled "Big data: double-edged sword". You should write at least 150 words but no more than 200 words.

Unit 7 Artificial Intelligence

Part One Academic Reading Skills

Word-formation

Mastering the word-formation can help readers understand new words and multiply their vocabulary. English words are made up of two parts: stem and affix. Affixes can be divided into prefixes and suffixes. Some stems themselves can be used as independent words. Since both stem and affix are word components that contain certain meanings, different combinations of stem and affix will form new meanings.

Tips:

1. Guess the meaning of the word according to its prefix and suffix.

2. Infer the meaning of a compound word from its parts.

Part Two Passage Reading

Passage A What Is Artificial Intelligence?

Pre-reading Task

Directions: *Read the title and discuss the following questions in groups.*

1. Have you used AI products before?
2. What do you think of AI?

Artificial Intelligence (AI), is the ability of a digital computer or computer-controlled robot to perform tasks commonly associated with intelligent beings. The term is frequently applied to the project of developing systems endowed with the intellectual processes characteristic of humans, such as the ability to reason, discover meaning, generalize, or learn from past experience. Since the development of the digital computer in the 1940s, it has been demonstrated that computers can be programmed to carry out very complex tasks—as, for example, discovering proofs for mathematical theorems or playing chess—with great proficiency. Still, despite continuing advances in computer processing speed and memory capacity, there are as yet no programs that can match human flexibility over wider domains or in tasks requiring much everyday knowledge. On the other hand, some programs have attained the performance levels of human experts and professionals in performing certain specific tasks, so that artificial intelligence in this limited sense is found in applications as diverse as medical diagnosis, computer search engines, and voice or handwriting recognition.

What Is Intelligence?

All but the simplest human behaviour is ascribed to intelligence, while even the most complicated insect behaviour is never taken as an indication of intelligence. What is the difference? Consider the behaviour of the digger wasp, Sphex ichneumoneus. When the female wasp returns to her burrow with food, she first deposits it on the threshold, checks for intruders inside her burrow, and only then, if the coast is clear, carries her food inside. The real nature of the wasp's instinctual behaviour is revealed if the food is moved a few inches away from the entrance to her burrow while she is inside: on emerging, she will repeat the whole procedure as often as the food is displaced. Intelligence—conspicuously absent in the case of Sphex—must include the ability to adapt to new circumstances.

Psychologists generally do not characterize human intelligence by just one trait but by the combination of many diverse abilities. Research in AI has focused chiefly on the following components of intelligence: learning, reasoning, problem solving, perception, and using language.

Learning

There are a number of different forms of learning as applied to artificial intelligence. The simplest is learning by trial and error. For example, a simple computer program for solving mate-in-one chess problems might try moves at random until mate is found. The program might then store the solution with the position so that the next time the computer encountered the same position it would recall the solution. This simple memorizing of individual items and procedures—known as rote learning—is relatively easy to implement on a computer. More challenging is the problem of implementing what is called generalization. Generalization involves applying past experience to analogous new situations. For example, a program that learns the past tense of regular English verbs by rote will not be able to produce the past tense of a word such as jump unless it previously had been presented with jumped, whereas a program that is able to generalize can learn the "added" rule and so form the past tense of jump based on experience with similar verbs.

Reasoning

To reason is to draw inferences appropriate to the situation. Inferences are classified as either deductive or inductive. An example of the former is, "Fred must be in either the museum or the café. He is not in the café; therefore he is in the museum," and of the latter, "Previous accidents of this sort were caused by instrument failure; therefore this accident was caused by instrument failure." The most significant difference between these forms of reasoning is that in the deductive case the truth of the premises guarantees the truth of the conclusion, whereas in the inductive case the truth of the premise lends support to the conclusion without giving absolute assurance. Inductive reasoning is common in science, where data are collected and tentative models are developed to describe and predict future behaviour—until the appearance of anomalous data forces the model to be revised. Deductive reasoning is common in mathematics and logic, where elaborate structures of irrefutable theorems are built up from a small set of basic axioms and rules.

There has been considerable success in programming computers to draw inferences, especially deductive inferences. However, true reasoning involves more than just drawing inferences; it involves drawing inferences relevant to the solution of the particular task or situation. This is one of the hardest problems confronting AI.

Problem Solving

Problem solving, particularly in artificial intelligence, may be characterized as a systematic search through a range of possible actions in order to reach some predefined goal or solution. Problem-solving methods divide into special purpose and general purpose. A special-purpose method is tailor-made for a particular problem and often exploits very specific features of the situation in which the problem is embedded. In contrast, a general-purpose method is applicable to a wide variety of problems. One general-purpose technique used in AI is means-end analysis—a step-by-step, or incremental, reduction of the difference between the current state and the final goal. The program selects actions from a list of means—in the case of a simple robot this might consist of PICK UP, PUT DOWN, MOVE FORWARD, MOVE BACK, MOVE LEFT, and MOVE RIGHT—until the goal is reached.

Many diverse problems have been solved by artificial intelligence programs. Some examples are finding the winning move (or sequence of moves) in a board game, devising mathematical proofs, and manipulating "virtual objects" in a computer-generated world.

Perception

In perception the environment is scanned by means of various sensory organs, real or artificial, and the scene is decomposed into separate objects in various spatial relationships. Analysis is complicated by the fact that an object may appear different depending on the angle from which it is viewed, the direction and intensity of illumination in the scene, and how much the object contrasts with the surrounding field.

At present, artificial perception is sufficiently well advanced to enable optical sensors to identify individuals, autonomous vehicles to drive at moderate speeds on the open road, and robots to roam through buildings collecting empty soda cans. One of the earliest systems to integrate perception and action was FREDDY, a stationary robot with a moving television eye and a pincer hand, constructed at the University of Edinburgh, Scotland, during the period 1966-1973 under the direction of Donald Michie. FREDDY was able to recognize a variety of objects and could be instructed to assemble simple artifacts, such as a toy car, from a random heap of components.

Language

A language is a system of signs having meaning by convention. In this sense, language need not be confined to the spoken word. Traffic signs, for example, form a minilanguage, it being a matter of convention that means "hazard ahead" in some countries. It is distinctive of languages that linguistic units possess meaning by convention, and linguistic meaning is very different from what is called natural meaning, exemplified in statements such as "Those clouds mean rain" and "The fall in pressure means the valve is malfunctioning."

An important characteristic of full-fledged human languages—in contrast to birdcalls and traffic signs—is their productivity. A productive language can formulate an unlimited variety of sentences.

It is relatively easy to write computer programs that seem able, in severely restricted contexts, to respond fluently in a human language to questions and statements. Although none of these programs actually understands language, they may, in principle, reach the point where their command of a language is indistinguishable from that of a normal human. What, then, is involved in genuine understanding, if even a computer that uses language like a native human speaker is not acknowledged to understand? There is no universally agreed upon answer to this difficult question. According to one theory, whether or not one understands depends not only on one's behaviour but also on one's history: in order to be said to understand, one must have learned the language and have been trained to take one's place in the linguistic community by means of interaction with other language users.

(Total words:1376, taken from: https://www.britannica.com)

Unit 7 Artificial Intelligence

New Words and Expressions

intellectual /ˌɪntəˈlektʃuəl/ adj. relating to the ability to understand things and think intelligently 智力的，聪明的，理智的

generalize /ˈdʒenərəlaɪz/ v. to form a general principle or opinion after considering only a small number of facts or examples 概括，推广，使…一般化

theorem /ˈθɪərəm/ n. a statement in mathematics or logic that can be proved to be true by reasoning 定理

proficiency /prəˈfɪʃ(ə)nsɪ/ n. the quality of having great facility and competence; skillfulness in the command of fundamentals deriving from practice and familiarity 精通，熟练

burrow /ˈbʌrəʊ/ n. a hole in the ground made by an animal for shelter 洞穴，地道 v. move through by or as by digging 探索，寻找，挖掘

analogous /əˈnæləgəs/ adj. similar to another situation or thing so that a comparison can be made 类似的

deductive /dɪˈdʌktɪv/ adj. using the knowledge and information you have in order to understand or form an opinion about something 推论的，推断的，演绎的

inductive /ɪnˈdʌktɪv/ adj. using known facts to produce general principles 归纳的，归纳法的

axiom /ˈæksɪəm/ n. a rule or principle that is generally considered to be true 公理

incremental /ˌɪnkrɪˈmentəl/ adj. increasing gradually by regular degrees or additions 增加的，增值的

Proper Nouns

AI   Artificial Intelligence   人工智能

the University of Edinburgh, Scotland   苏格兰爱丁堡大学

Reading Task

Task 1 Complete the following table about the main points of the text.

Artificial intelligence	All but the simplest _____ is ascribed to intelligence, while even the most complicated insect behaviour is never taken as an indication of _____.
	Research in AI has focused chiefly on the following components of intelligence: learning, reasoning, _____, perception, and using _____.
	There are a number of different forms of learning as applied to artificial intelligence. The simplest is _____. More challenging is _____.
	To reason is to draw inferences appropriate to the situation. Inferences are classified as either _____ or _____.
	Problem solving, particularly in artificial intelligence, may be characterized as a systematic search through a range of possible actions in order to reach some _____.
	In perception the environment is scanned by _____, and the scene is decomposed into _____.
	A language is a _____ having meaning by convention.

Task 2 Decide whether the following statements are true (T) or false (F).

1. There has been considerable success in programming computers to

draw inferences, especially deductive inferences. (　　)

2. Problem-solving methods divide into special purpose and general purpose. (　　)

3. One general-purpose technique used in AI is means-end analysis—a step-by-step, or incremental, reduction of the difference between the current state and the final goal. (　　)

4. A language is a system of signs having meaning by convention. In this sense, language need not be confined to the spoken word. (　　)

5. A productive language can formulate an unlimited variety of sentences. (　　)

6. What, then, is involved in genuine understanding if a computer that uses language like a native human speaker is not acknowledged to understand? There is a universally agreed upon answer to this difficult question. (　　)

7. Many diverse problems have been solved by artificial perception programs. (　　)

Task 3 Group discussion.

With the rapid development of AI, here are two opinions associated with the influences it has brought us. Work in groups of 3—4 and come up with other points of view as many as possible.

It makes our life more convenient and colorful.

It will break our plate someday.

Task 4 Work in pairs and answer the following questions.

1. What are the disadvantages of AI programs up to now, even

though there are increasing developments in computer processing speed and memory capacity?

2. What are the most significant difference between the deductive form of reasoning and the inductive one?

3. How is the environment scanned in perception according to the author?

4. What is an important characteristic of human languages in contrast to birdcalls and traffic signs?

Language Building-up

Task 1 The following expressions are taken from Text A. Translate the following terms from English into Chinese.

computer-controlled robot

memory capacity

medical diagnosis

voice or handwriting recognition

adapt to new circumstances

rote learning

systematic search

instrument failure

be confined to

linguistic units

Task 2 Complete the following sentences with the correct form of the words in the box.

> intellectual generalize theorem proficiency
> burrow analogous deductive inductive

1. It is in this context that one runs across the fundamental _____ of arithmetic and arithmetic functions.

2. An _____ argument is such that the truth of their premises makes the conclusion more or less probable.

3. There is nothing preventing her from dragging the cricket into the _____ if she chooses to do so.

4. High levels of lead could damage the _____ development of children.

5. This paper reports the effects of L2 writing knowledge and free compositions on Chinese university students English writing _____.

6. It's impossible to _____ about children's books, as they are all different.

7. John Mearsheimer's offensive realism is noted for its delicate _____ logic and bold theoretical conclusion on international politics.

8. The relationship of a teacher and his students is _____ to that of a director and the actors.

Task 3 Translate the following paragraph into English.

人工智能是一门极富挑战性的科学,从事这项工作的人必须懂得计算机知识、心理学和哲学。它由不同的领域组成,如机器学习、计算机视觉等。总的说来,人工智能研究的一个主要目标是使机器能够胜任一些通常需要人类智能才能完成的复杂工作。人工智能从诞生以来,理论和技术日益成熟,应用领域也不断扩大,可以设想,未来人工智能带来的科技产品,将会是人类智慧的"容器"。

Passage B Benefits & Risks of Artificial Intelligence

From SIRI to self-driving cars, artificial intelligence (AI) is progressing rapidly. While science fiction often portrays AI as robots with human-like characteristics, AI can encompass anything from Google's search algorithms to IBM's Watson to autonomous weapons.

Artificial intelligence today is properly known as narrow AI (or weak AI), in that it is designed to perform a narrow task (e.g. only facial recognition or only internet searches or only driving a car). However, the long-term goal of many researchers is to create general AI (AGI or strong AI). While narrow AI may outperform humans at whatever its specific task is, like playing chess or solving equations, AGI would outperform humans at nearly every cognitive task.

Why research AI safety?

In the near term, the goal of keeping AI's impact on society beneficial motivates research in many areas, from economics and law to technical topics such as verification, validity, security and control. Whereas it may be little more than a minor nuisance if your laptop crashes or gets hacked, it becomes all the more important that an AI system does what you want it to do if it controls your car, your airplane, your pacemaker, your automated trading system or your power grid. Another short-term challenge is preventing a devastating arms race in lethal autonomous weapons.

In the long term, an important question is what will happen if the quest for strong AI succeeds and an AI system becomes better than humans at all cognitive tasks. As pointed out by I. J. Good in 1965, designing smarter AI systems is itself a cognitive task. Such a system could potentially undergo recursive self-improvement, triggering an intelligence explosion leaving human intellect far behind. By inventing revolutionary new technologies, such a superintelligence might help us eradicate war, disease, and poverty, and so the creation of strong AI might be the biggest event in human history. Some experts have expressed concern, though, that it might also be the last, unless we learn to align the goals of the AI with ours before it becomes superintelligent.

There are some who question whether strong AI will ever be achieved, and others who insist that the creation of superintelligent AI is guaranteed to be beneficial. At FLI we recognize both of these possibilities, but also recognize the potential for an artificial intelligence system to intentionally or unintentionally cause great harm. We believe research today will help us better prepare for and prevent such potentially negative consequences in the future, thus enjoying the benefits of AI while avoiding pitfalls.

How can AI be dangerous?

Most researchers agree that a superintelligent AI is unlikely to exhibit human emotions like love or hate, and that there is no reason to expect AI to become intentionally benevolent or malevolent. Instead, when considering how AI might become a risk, experts think two scenarios most likely:

The AI is programmed to do something devastating: Autonomous weapons are artificial intelligence systems that are programmed to kill. In the hands of the wrong person, these weapons could easily cause mass casualties. Moreover, an AI arms race could inadvertently lead to an AI war that also results in mass casualties. To avoid being thwarted by the enemy, these weapons would be designed to be extremely difficult to simply "turn off", so humans could plausibly lose control of such a situation. This risk is one that's present even with narrow AI, but grows as levels of AI intelligence and autonomy increase.

The AI is programmed to do something beneficial, but it develops a destructive method for achieving its goal: This can happen whenever we fail to fully align the AI's goals with ours, which is strikingly difficult. If you ask an obedient intelligent car to take you to the airport as fast as possible, it might get you there chased by helicopters and covered in vomit, doing not what you wanted but literally what you asked for. If a superintelligent system is tasked with an ambitious geoengineering project, it might wreak havoc with our ecosystem as a side effect, and view human attempts to stop it as a threat to be met.

As these examples illustrate, the concern about advanced AI isn't malevolence but competence. A super-intelligent AI will be extremely good at accomplishing its goals, and if those goals aren't aligned with ours, we have a problem. You're probably not an evil ant-hater who steps on ants out of malice, but if you're in charge of a hydroelectric green energy project and there's an anthill in the region to be flooded, too bad for the ants. A key goal of AI safety research is to never place humanity in the position of those ants.

Why the recent interest in AI safety?

Stephen Hawking, Elon Musk, Steve Wozniak, Bill Gates, and many other big names in science and technology have recently expressed concern in the media and via open letters about the risks posed by AI, joined by many leading AI researchers. Why is the subject suddenly in the headlines?

The idea that the quest for strong AI would ultimately succeed was long thought of as science fiction, centuries or more away. However, thanks to recent breakthroughs, many AI milestones, which experts viewed as decades away merely five years ago, have now been reached, making many experts take seriously the possibility of superintelligence in our lifetime. While some experts still guess that human-level AI is centuries away, most AI researches at the 2015 Puerto Rico Conference guessed that it would happen before 2060. Since it may take decades to complete the required safety research, it is prudent to start it now.

Because AI has the potential to become more intelligent than any human, we have no surefire way of predicting how it will behave. We can't use past technological developments as much of a basis because we've never created anything that has the ability to, wittingly or unwittingly, outsmart us. The best example of what we could face may be our own evolution. People now control the planet, not because we're the strongest, fastest or biggest, but because we're the smartest. If we're no longer the smartest, are we assured to remain in control?

FLI's position is that our civilization will flourish as long as we win the race between the growing power of technology and the wisdom with which we manage it. In the case of AI technology, FLI's position is that the best way to win that race is not to impede the former, but to accelerate the latter, by supporting AI safety research.

(Total words:1129, taken from: https://futureoflife.org/)

New Words and Expressions

encompass /ɪnˈkʌmpəs/ v. include in scope;include as part of something broader;have as one's sphere or territory 包含;包围,环绕;完成

equation /ɪˈkweʃən/ n. a mathematical statement that two expressions are equal 方程式,等式

verification /verɪfɪˈkeɪʃ(ə)n/ n. additional proof that something that was believed (some fact or hypothesis or theory) is correct 确认,查证;核实

devastating /ˈdevəsteɪtɪŋ/ adj. badly damaging or destroying something 毁灭性的

recursive /rɪˈkɜːsɪv/ adj. of or relating to a recursion (数)递归的,循环的

triggering /ˈtrɪɡərɪŋ/ n. a device that activates or releases or causes something to happen（电子）触发；起动 v. put in motion or move to act 引起（trigger 的 ing 形式）

eradicate /ɪˈrædɪkeɪt/ v. destroy completely, as if down to the roots; kill in large numbers 根除，根绝；消灭

hydroelectric /ˌhaɪdrəʊɪˈlektrɪk/ adj. of or relating to or used in the production of electricity by water power 水力发电的，水电治疗的

unwittingly /ʌnˈwɪtɪŋli/ adv. without knowledge or intention 不知不觉地，不知情地，不经意地

superintelligent /ˌsjuːpərɪnˈtelɪdʒənt/ adj. 有超常智慧的

Proper Nouns

SIRI　iPhone 上的语音控制功能

IBM　美国国际商用机器公司

AGI　美国地质学会

Reading Task

Task 1　Work in pairs and answer the following questions.

1. How to understand that AI is a double-edged sword?

2. The AI is programmed to do something devastating and beneficial. Which specific aspects does it include?

3. Why is the recent interest in AI safety?

4. "A key goal of AI safety research is to never place humanity in the position of those ants."(Para. 9) What does this sentence mean?

Language Building-up

Task 1 Translate the following sentences from the passage into Chinese.

1. Artificial intelligence today is properly known as narrow AI, in that it is designed to perform a narrow task.

2. In the near term, the goal of keeping AI's impact on society beneficial motivates research in many areas, from economics and law to technical topics such as verification, validity, security and control.

3. As these examples illustrate, the concern about advanced AI isn't malevolence but competence.

4. This risk is one that's present even with narrow AI, but grows as levels of AI intelligence and autonomy increase.

5. However, the long-term goal of many researchers is to create general AI (AGI or strong AI).

Task 2 Paraphrase the following sentences from the passage.

1. While narrow AI may outperform humans at whatever its specific task is, like playing chess or solving equations, AGI would outperform humans at nearly every cognitive task.

2. Such a system could potentially undergo recursive self-improvement, triggering an intelligence explosion leaving human intellect far behind.

3. There are some who question whether strong AI will ever be achieved, and others who insist that the creation of superintelligent AI is guaranteed to be beneficial.

4. However, thanks to recent breakthroughs, many AI milestones, which experts viewed as decades away merely five years ago, have now been reached, making many experts take seriously the possibility of superintelligence in our lifetime.

Part Three Academic Writing

Theme-related Writing

On the basis of what you have learned from this unit, write an essay entitled "Should we be afraid of AI?". You should write at least 150 words but no more than 200 words.

Unit 8 Virtual Environment

Part One Academic Reading Skills

Understanding Transitions

Transition is a kind of relational guideline. It is the link between sentences and sentences, paragraphs and paragraphs. Whether the passage is written consistently depends largely on the understanding of transitions.

Tips:

1. Look through the pages of your reading passage and read the headings of the chapter.

2. Read the passage carefully. If there are ideas that seem important, make a note on paper.

3. Take time to reflect on what you have read. Find the transitions to help you understand the structure of the passage.

4. Consider the main points of the passage and summarize the passage using your own words.

Part Two Passage Reading

Passage A   Virtual Reality

Pre-reading Task

Directions: *Read the title and discuss the following questions in groups*.

1. What do you know about virtual reality (VR)? Do you know how VR works?

2. Can you list some applications of virtual reality?

While pressing the keys of your keyboard or keypad to convert the lost games to last moment victories the chances are you have encountered the virtual reality in your life. These games involve you with the characters or objects and with the amplification of the involvement, which makes one feel a part of this virtual world. By using 3D imagery with a head-mounted device (HMD) and high-quality surrounding sound equipment, these games create more involvement in the virtual world and consequently shut down the cues of real world. This is called virtual reality, which has applications far beyond gaming.

What Is Virtual Reality?

Virtual reality can be defined as an upcoming technology that makes users feel in a Virtual Environment (VE) by using computer hardware and software. It was originally conceived as a digitally created space which humans could access by donning special computer equipments. It enables people to deal with information more easily. VR provides a different way to see and experience information, one that is dynamic and immediate. For example, in a computer game, user's joystick motions are tracked and the objects in the game are moved according to the joystick movements. In the same way a simulated, three-dimensional world is created around the user in which he/she could interact with objects, people, and environments. Typically three-dimensional life-sized images with support of audio devices are presented around the user and the perspective is modified in accordance with the user input (generally head or eye movements). Many devices along with the computers are used to create a virtual environment.

How VR Works

A simple example of "Counter Strike" game can give a thought as to how virtual reality works. The software program for the game is the major element which runs with the help of the computer system and the interfaced input-output devices. Every character and environment within the game behaves closely to reality as per the code written for them. The code facilitates characters and environment to interact with the other characters controlled by the input devices. The code is interpreted by the processor which handles the input-output devices accordingly. This is the simplest example of how VR works. The working of more immersive virtual reality environment is quite similar to working of the game besides the fact that a number of advanced input and output devices along with a high performance processor are added to increase the immersion.

The processor executes the processes quickly according to the input given by the user and output is presented to the user in a way that user feels itself a part of the environment and its objects. The video below shows an example of more immersive virtual reality.

The 3D visualization component enables the user to see 3D scenarios by using a display methodology like a head-mounted device. Typically the 3D images superimpose the real environment by using one of the displays, screen-based or projection-based. The screen-based virtual environment generally uses a high-quality display screen in terms of resolution and color, or a head-mounted device along with the sound system as output devices. A keyboard, microphone, head tracking sensors, finger trackers, gesture recognition system, a joystick or similar gears are used as input devices. When user moves the gear or joystick, make move of the head, or press any key on the keyboard, the objects of the screen are changed accordingly in a way that user feels if he/she is directly controlling the objects and environments on the screen. A high-speed powerful processor processes the inputs. An Application Programming Interface (API) provides the interface to the input devices connected to the system as well as to standard devices like mouse and keyboard. The timings and relationship between input and output devices are so perfect that user feels an immersion with the virtual environment.

The other technique used to create a virtual environment is projection-based, which is more immersive than the screen-based method. The display images are projected on the multi-screen spaces ranging from two to six screens. A six-screen's would make a better virtual environment. Both floor and ceiling use a rear projection while the other four screens yield large surrounding views for both panning actions and looking down. Consequently, objects inside the space could be walked around and virtual entreat could be touched.

Head-Mounted Display & CAVE

VR Environments: Head Mounted Display

The most commonly used hardware equipment in virtual reality technology is HMD which renders the virtual environment in front of eyes. A HMD provides full color quality viewing with clear, vivid graphics and stunning imagery. The device can connect to any computer or video source via an SVGA or DVI connection. They have integrated headphones to deliver the full stereo surround sounds.

A typical Head-Mounted Device incorporates two miniature display screens and an optical system that channels the images from screens to the eyes, presenting a stereo viewing of the virtual world.

A motion tracker continuously records the position and orientation of the user's head and eyeballs, and allows the image generating computer to adjust the scene representation to the current view. Resultantly, users are able to look around or walk through the surroundings of the virtual environment. The head orientation is generally tracked through a device, such as accelerometer which provides the feedback regarding the pitch, yaw and roll of the user's head. To track the user's movement in the physical space, optical or magnetic trackers are attached with the user to record the information about the X, Y and Z coordinates of the user's position.

VR Environments: CAVE (Cave Automatic Virtual Environment)

CAVE, Cave Automatic Virtual Environment, is another immersive VE system which projects images on the walls, floor and ceiling of a room. It generally uses multiple cameras and a projection screen in an enclosed room to make users feel that they are surrounded by a virtual environment. The more complex CAVEs use hardware that creates a different sensory model that is beyond the physical stimuli, such as the auditory aspects of a virtual environment which can be transmitted through headphones or speakers. The sound interacts with the brain three-dimensionally enhancing the realism of the virtual environment experience. The sense of touch is also incorporated in the CAVEs by using sensory gloves and other haptic devices. Some haptic devices also allow users to exert a touch or grasp or replace a virtual object.

Applications

As Virtual Reality has gained traction in the real world, scientists and researchers have started to think about their use in various fields like medical science, gaming and education.

Medical Science—One of the most common uses of the virtual reality is in Virtual Reality Exposure Therapy (VRET) which treats the patients suffering from some specific anxiety or phobias. Patients are gradually introduced to the negative situations in a virtual environment until they become desensitized and are able to handle with their fear or anxiety. The diseases like acrophobia (the fear of heights), agoraphobia (fear of spaces), arachnophobia (social phobia) are treated using the VERT therapy. Virtual Environments (VEs) are also used to study the patient's reactions and behaviors to high anxiety environments. Medical students, doctors and nurses are taught the basics of human anatomy as well as surgical procedures by creating 3D virtual models.

Education—Virtual Reality is used to train people working in widely diverse settings or professions, from fighter pilots to librarians. The simulation of environments using sensory immersion has been proven an effective training method. Training in monitoring and verification of performance is as simple as simulating the normal and abnormal conditions within the workplace environment. Simulations can be distributed to centers to be used by the trainers or trainees, and new environments and conditions can be added easily. The use of virtual reality is also increasing in military, especially to train pilots by developing special flight simulators which provide pilots a safer and less expensive way to learn flying skills. Also virtual simulations of conflict scenarios have been used to teach soldiers how to make quick and effective decisions under stressful circumstances. An example of a simulation tool is "Maxwell World", which is designed to help students understand the concepts of electrostatic fields. Generally students have trouble understanding the relationship of abstractions about electric fields to phenomenological dynamics. The Maxwell World enable learners to virtually experience scientifically accurate models of electric fields and make factors significant that are not noticeable in the real world like how forces at each point in space continually accelerate a test charge through 3D interactive imageries.

Gaming—Gaming is another industry where virtual reality technology is deployed and resultantly we have more interactive and entertaining games with us. These 3D games use a high definition helmet mounted with LCD or LED screen and 3D stereo headset. The gamers are highly immersed with the gaming scenario and the characters and objects interact with the gamer like live things. Some companies like Sony are now involved in developing games augmented with the VR technology.

(Total words: 1494, taken from: https://www.engineersgarage.com/articles/virtual-reality-environment)

New Words and Expressions

amplification /ˌæmplɪfɪˈkeɪʃən/ n. the amount of increase in signal power or voltage or current expressed as the ratio of output to input（电子）放大（率），扩大，详述

mount /maʊnt/ n. something forming a back that is added for strengthening 山峰；底座；乘骑用马；攀，登；运载工具；底座

cue /kjuː/ n. evidence that helps to solve a problem 提示，暗示；线索

immersive /ɪˈmɜːsɪv/ adj. providing information or stimulation for a number of senses, not only sight and sound 拟真的;沉浸式的,沉浸感的;增加沉浸感的

execute /ˈeksɪkjuːt/ vt. put in effect 实行,执行;处死

superimpose /ˌsuːpərɪmˈpəuz/ vt. place on top of 添加,重叠,附加,安装

joystick /ˈdʒɔɪstɪk/ n. a manual control consisting of a vertical handle that can move freely in two directions; used as an input device to computers or to devices controlled by computers 操纵杆,(机)控制杆

entreat /ɪnˈtriːt/ vt. ask for or request earnestly 恳求,请求

stun /stʌn/ vt. make senseless or dizzy by or as if by a blow 使震惊;打昏;给以深刻的印象

pitch /pɪtʃ/ n. 沥青;音高;程度;树脂;倾斜;投掷;球场

yaw /jɔː/ n. an erratic deflection from an intended course(火箭、飞机、宇宙飞船等)偏航

haptic /ˈhæptɪk/ adj. of or relating to or proceeding from the sense of touch 触觉的

desensitize /diˈsensətaɪz/ vt. make insensitive 使不敏感,使麻木不仁

acrophobia /ˌækrəˈfəubɪə/ n. a morbid fear of great heights 恐高症,高处恐怖症

agoraphobia /ˌægərəˈfəubɪə/ n. a morbid fear of open spaces (as fear of being caught alone in some public place) 旷野恐怖;(心理)广场恐怖症;陌生环境恐怖症

phobia /ˈfəubɪə/ n. an anxiety disorder characterized by extreme and irrational fear of simple things or social situations 恐怖,憎恶;恐惧症

anatomy /əˈnætəmi/ n. the branch of morphology that deals with the structure of animals 解剖；解剖学；剖析；骨骼

electrostatic /ɪˌlektrəʊˈstætɪk/ adj. concerned with or producing or caused by static electricity 静电的，静电学的

phenomenological /fiˌnɑːmɪnəˈlɑːdʒɪkəl/ adj. 现象的，现象学的

deploy /dɪˈplɔɪ/ vt. to distribute systematically or strategically 配置；展开；使疏开

helmet /ˈhelmɪt/ n. a protective headgear made of hard material to resist blows 钢盔，头盔

component /kəmˈpəʊnənt/ n. an abstract part of something 成分；组件；（电子）元件

scenarios /sɪˈnɑːrɪəʊz/ n. a setting for a work of art or literature 情节；脚本；情景介绍（scenario 的复数）

methodology /meθəˈdɑːlədʒi/ n. the branch of philosophy that analyzes the principles and procedures of inquiry in a particular discipline 方法学，方法论

rear /rɪə/ adj. the side of an object that is opposite its front 后方的，后面的，背面的

stereo /ˈsterɪəʊ/ adj. used to describe a sound system in which the sound is played through two speakers 立体的，立体声的，立体感觉的

miniature /ˈmɪnɪəʃə/ adj. used to describe something that is very small, especially a smaller version of something which is normally much bigger 微型的，小规模的

librarian /laɪˈbrerɪən/ n. a person who is in charge of a library or who has been specially trained to work in a library 图书馆员，图书管理员

arachnophobia /əˌræknəˈfəʊbɪə/ n. an abnormal fear of spiders 蜘蛛

恐惧症

Proper Nouns

  HMD Head Mount Display 头戴式显示器

  API Application Program Interface 应用程序接口

  CAVE Cave Automatic Virtual Environment 洞穴状自动虚拟系统

  VRET Virtual Reality Exposure Therapy 虚拟现实暴露疗法

Reading Task

Task 1 Work in pairs and answer the following questions.

1. Read the passage through quickly and think: What is called virtual reality?

2. According to the structure of the passage, can you summarize the main body based on understanding transitions?

3. Why is virtual reality widely used in education?

Task 2 Complete the following table about the main points of the text.

Virtual reality	What is Virtual Reality?	
	How does VR work?	
	Head-Mounted Display & CAVE	
	Applications	

Task 3 Decide whether the following statements are true (T) or false (F).

1. The code is interpreted by the software program which handles the input-output devices accordingly. (   )

2. The 3D visualization component enables the user to see 3D scenarios by using a display methodology like a head-mounted device. (   )

3. It generally uses one camera and a projection screen in an enclosed room to make users feel that they are surrounded by a virtual environment. (   )

4. The sound interacts with the brain three dimensionally enhancing the realism of the virtual environment experience. (   )

5. The sense of touch is also incorporated in the CAVEs by using sensory gloves and other haptic devices. (   )

6. Medical students, doctors and nurses are taught the basics of human anatomy as well as surgical procedures by creating 2D virtual models. (   )

7. Simulations can be distributed to centers to be used by the trainers or trainees, and new environments and conditions can be added easily. (   )

Task 4 Work in pairs and answer the following questions.

1. "The software program for the game is the major element which runs with the help of the computer system and the interfaced input-output devices."(Para. 3) What does "*which*" refer to?

2. "The processor executes the processes quickly according to the

input given by the user and output is presented to the user in a way that user feels itself a part of the environment and its objects." (Para. 3) Why does the author use two parallel passive voices in this sentence?

3. "A keyboard, microphone, head tracking sensors, finger trackers, gesture recognition system, a joystick or similar gears are used as input devices."(Para. 3) Why does the author mention so many input devices?

4. How many applications are mentioned in this passage? What are they?

5. How are the auditory aspects of a virtual environment transmitted?

Task 5 Group Discussion

With the development of virtual reality, there are an increasing number of fields using VR technology. Here are two opinions associated with the VR application in medical science. Work in groups of 3—4 and come up with other points of view as many as possible.

Virtual reality can treat patients suffering from some specific anxiety or phobias.

Virtual reality may not be accurate enough in medical field.

Language Building-up

Task 1 The following expressions are taken from Text A. Translate the following terms from English into Chinese.

head-mounted device

3D imagery

interfaced input and output devices

3D visualization component

finger trackers

gesture recognition system

application programming interface

full stereo surround sounds

virtual reality exposure therapy

high-definition helmet

Task 2 Complete the following sentences with the correct form of the words in the box.

immersive   superimpose   interface   amplification
yaw   joystick   electrostatic   haptic

1. When you complete the installation, you can use these basic concepts and architecture descriptions to build your own _____ environments, games, or next-generation computing interfaces.

2. Visual displays incorporated into the retina of our eyes, direct conductance "speakers" implanted in our ears, and _____ sensors incorporated into our fingertips.

3. The opposing _____ and van der Waals forces are typically balanced for film thicknesses in the range of 10-1000 nm.

4. Drivers use a _____ of sorts to steer and throttle the vehicle, which can spin in place and accelerate rather quickly.

5. As the plane climbed to 370 feet, it started _____.

6. This sense of _____ suggests that the worst is expected.

7. He had _____ all this machinery with a master computer.

8. Patterns of public administration and government are _____ on traditional societies.

Task 3 Translate the following paragraph into English.

它通常在一个封闭的房间里使用多个摄像头和投影屏幕，让用户感觉到他们被虚拟环境包围。更复杂的洞穴状自动虚拟系统使用硬件来创建一个不同的感官模型，这个模型超越了物理刺激，例如虚拟环境的听觉方面可以通过耳机或扬声器传输。声音与大脑的三维互动增强了虚拟环境体验的真实性。通过使用感觉手套和其他触觉装置，触觉也被融入到洞穴状自动虚拟系统中。一些触觉设备还允许用户触摸、抓取或替换虚拟物体。

Passage B   How Reality Technology Is Used in Business?

Virtual reality has become big business, and its mainstream availability is one of those rare, genuinely exciting developments that can't help but spark the imagination. The entertainment aspects of VR, as well as its cousins—augmented reality and mixed reality, are the most obvious. Traveling far and wide to places real or imagined, flying through space, and interacting with fantastical creatures are the kinds of VR that come to mind most readily.

Entertainment isn't the only area where virtual reality is making an impact, though. Thought leaders in the business world saw the potential early on for workplace productivity applications, and developers are working hard to bring them to market.

Applications of Virtual and Augmented Reality in Business

Although the field is still new, it is clear that virtual reality will change the way we do business. The only question is when, and who will be at the forefront of the revolution. Here are just a few of the ways that virtual reality and related technologies might impact the office in days to come.

VR Remote Training Employees

With the rise of the Internet and remote work, today's organizations are more geographically dispersed than ever before. Employees working on the same team might not report to the same office. They might not live in the same city, or even the same country. Although this trend has led to wonderful gains in productivity and employee satisfaction, it does have its downside. According to the Association for Talent Development (ATD), businesses spend an average of $1,208 per employee training them in the skills required to do their job. Almost 2/3 of the cost is attributed to tangential expenses like instructor travel, the development of training courses, and other costs not related directly to instructor pay.

Utilizing VR in the training infrastructure could reduce these costs while increasing the effectiveness of training. In the virtual world, a single instructor could teach a single classroom consisting of new employees spread all over the world. The technology is unaffected by physical distance, and the natural interactions it affords have been shown to be more engaging than a phone call or video conference. Training courses and simulations benefit from VR as well. For employees learning complex tasks using machinery, or learning how to deal with unexpected situations, a virtual environment provides valuable practical experience.

Mixed Reality Data Organization

Life often imitates art. More specifically, technology often imitates science fiction. The modern Internet was predicted by William Gibson and other cyberpunk writers soon after the advent of the first computer networks. The first cell phones were inspired by the handheld communicators used in Star Trek, with later flip phones even modeled on them aesthetically. One innovation that is often seen in popular media, but not yet delivered in the real world, is the floating user interface. Think about Minority Report, or Tony Stark tinkering away on his Iron Man suit designs. The manipulation of data using natural, instinctive hand motions has obvious efficiency benefits.

In fact, the science consultant behind Minority Report recently built Mezzanine. This is a dedicated mixed reality room that makes good on those concepts. His firm is pitching it to large corporations as a collaboration solution. For those of us who don't have access to that kind of space and budget, virtual reality and augmented reality headsets will offer the next best thing. VR could provide an easy way to transport the user entirely into their work, a space filled with data and charts and images to manipulate. AR might be even more practical, integrating hand-written notes, printed documents, and physical objects into the interface.

Virtual Reality Communication and Collaboration

The best aspect of virtual reality, at least from the standpoint of workplace productivity, is its geographical agnosticism. Everything that makes it effective for employee training purposes works just as well for collaboration. Team members located around the world could meet in a virtual conference room, pointing and gesturing and using natural body language to communicate. Of course, there's no reason the conference room has to be a conference room. The team could just as easily meet on top of Mount Everest, in the Oval Office, or in outer space. The virtual environment can serve to focus employees, set the mood, or just provide a welcome change of scenery.

It's true for individual workers as well. Collaboration is a way of life in today's workforce, but everyone sometimes feels the need to concentrate on their work without the noise and distractions of their co-workers. Virtual reality can provide this, letting workers slip away into their own world and their own to-do list. In the future, it might not be uncommon to see a physically open office where some of the more solitary employees have entered their own virtual cubicles.

Three Real-World Examples of VR and AR in the Workplace

Although the productivity VR and AR space is largely wide-open, a few solutions have already come to market. As with most things related to virtual reality, they are exciting glimpses of what will be possible as the technology advances and adoption spreads.

Google Translate

With the 2015 acquisition of Word Lens and the integration of its existing and very powerful translation engine, Google created one of the most stunning augmented reality applications available today. Google Translate, free for iOS and Android, seems like magic the first time one sees it work. Using the camera on a mobile device, the App provides a real-time translation of text in the real world. The uses for this are innumerable. Point the phone at a restaurant menu in Spanish, and it will appear in English on the screen. It works just as well for letters, or packing slips, or instruction manuals. The App currently supports 29 languages with the real-time functionality, and 37 using still photos.

Virtual Desktop

One of the simplest but most effective uses of VR to date, the Virtual Desktop app for Oculus Rift and HTC Vive works exactly as it sounds. Slip on a supported head-mounted display, and the Windows desktop appears before you, floating in space. The VR wrapper supports web browsers, video streaming, and even software like Microsoft Office. The most useful feature of Virtual Desktop is its ability to stretch the desktop almost infinitely far. App windows can be resized to incredible proportions, or moved far beyond the bounds of any monitor that exists in the real world. For the worker looking for a little more desktop space, this is without a doubt the best solution currently available.

LiveViewRift

Also available for Oculus Rift or Samsung Gear VR is LiveViewRift. Conceived as a media player, the software allows locally stored video files, images, and video streaming sites like YouTube to be viewed directly on the head-mounted display. LiveViewRift offers distortion and field-of-view correction algorithms to fit traditional 2D media into the 3D space. For workplace productivity, and especially for training, LiveViewRift has another function that makes it incredibly valuable. The App is able to stream from any standard network camera supporting MJPG or a number of other common streaming protocols. Virtual attendance to seminars, training sessions, or workshops can be had for the price of a consumer-level head-mounted display. Virtual reality is booming, and more applications are released daily. Although the productivity field is not as crowded as other types of VR Apps, the potential for them to make a real impact on the way we work and live is truly enormous.

(Total words: 1255, taken from: https://www.realitytechnologies.com/applications/business/)

New Words and Expressions

genuinely /ˈdʒenjuinli/ adv. in accordance with truth or fact or reality 真诚地,诚实地

readily /ˈredɪli/ adv. without much difficulty 容易地;乐意地;无困难地

tangential /tænˈdʒenʃl/ adj. of or relating to or acting along or in the direction of a tangent (数) 切线的,正切的;离题的,扯远的

unaffected /ˌʌnəˈfektɪd/ adj. 不受影响的;自然的;真挚的;不矫揉造作的

imitate /ˈɪmɪteɪt/ vt. make a reproduction or copy of 模仿,仿效;仿造,仿制

cyberpunk /ˈsaɪbəpʌŋk/ n. a programmer who breaks into computer systems in order to steal or change or destroy information as a form of cyber-terrorism 网络朋客

handheld /hændheld/ adj. small and light enough to be operated while you hold it in your hands 掌上型,手持型

aesthetically /esˈθetɪklɪ/ adv. in a tasteful way 审美地;美学观点上地

tinker /ˈtɪŋkər/ v. do random, unplanned work or activities or spend time idly 笨拙的修补

mezzanine /ˈmezəniːn/ n. intermediate floor just above the ground floor 中层楼,夹楼

standpoint /ˈstændpɔɪnt/ n. a mental position from which things are viewed 立场,观点

agnosticism /æɡˈnɑːstɪsɪzəm/ n. the disbelief in any claims of ultimate knowledge 不可知论

cubicle /ˈkjuːbɪkl/ n. small area set off by walls for special use 小卧室;小隔间

innumerable /ɪˈnuːmərəbl/ adj. too numerous to be counted 无数的,数不清的

wrapper /ˈræpə/ n. the covering (usually paper or cellophane) in which something is wrapped 包装材料；(包装)包装纸；书皮

distortion /dɪsˈtɔːʃən/ n. a change (usually undesired) in the waveform of an acoustic or analog electrical signal; the difference between two measurements of a signal (as between the input and output signal) 变形；(物)失真；扭曲；曲解

seminar /ˈsemɪnɑːr/ n. any meeting for an exchange of ideas 讨论会，研讨班

Proper Nouns

ATD   Association for Talent Development   人才发展协会

Minority Report   少数派报告

Oval Office   美国总统办公室

Reading Task

Task 1 Work in pairs and answer the following questions.

1. "Virtual reality can provide this, letting workers slip away into their own world and their own to-do list."(Para. 9) What does "*this*" refer to according to the passage?

2. "... a virtual environment provides valuable practical experience." (Para. 5) What experience has virtual environment brought us?

3. How does Google Translate use VR technology? Have you ever used this technology? Share your experience with your partner.

Unit 8 Virtual Environment

Language Building-up

Task 1 Translate the following sentences from the passage into Chinese.

1. In the virtual world, a single instructor could teach a single classroom consisting of new employees spread all over the world.

2. The technology is unaffected by physical distance, and the natural interactions it affords have been shown to be more engaging than a phone call or video conference.

3. VR could provide an easy way to transport the user entirely into their work, a space filled with data and charts and images to manipulate.

4. As with most things related to virtual reality, they are exciting glimpses of what will be possible as the technology advances and adoption spreads.

Task 2 Paraphrase the following sentences from the passage.

1. Traveling far and wide to places real or imagined, flying through space, and interacting with fantastical creatures are the kinds of VR that

come to mind most readily.

_____

_____

2. For employees learning complex tasks using machinery, or learning how to deal with unexpected situations, a virtual environment provides valuable practical experience.

_____

_____

3. One innovation that is often seen in popular media, but not yet delivered in the real world, is the floating user interface.

_____

_____

4. Collaboration is a way of life in today's workforce, but everyone sometimes feels the need to concentrate on their work without the noise and distractions of their co-workers.

_____

_____

Part Three Academic Writing

Theme-related Writing

On the basis of what you have learned from this unit, write an essay entitled "Virtual reality: application in entertainment". You should write at least 150 words but no more than 200 words.